Beginner-Friendly
QUILTS

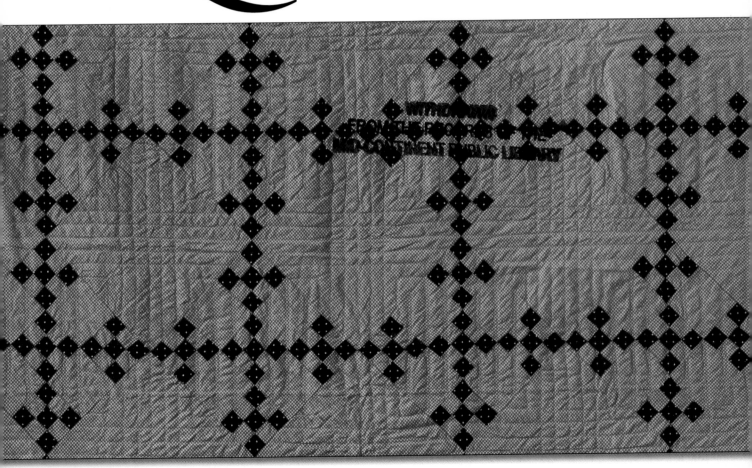

LEISURE ARTS, INC.
Little Rock, Arkansas

When a love of quilts becomes a love of quilting, it's an exciting thing! This collection of classic quilt designs offers twelve bed-size quilts and two baby quilts—each an excellent pattern choice for the first-time quilter. So that you experience greater accuracy and fast results, the instructions are for rotary-cutting methods. And most of the patterns have assembly and quilting diagrams to help you finish your first quilt with ease! Discover all the fun and satisfaction of re-creating these heirloom quilts for yourself and your loved ones.

editorial staff

editor-in-chief: Susan White Sullivan
craft publications director: Cheryl Johnson
special projects director: Susan Frantz Wiles
senior prepress director: Mark Hawkins
art publications director: Rhonda Shelby
technical writer: Lisa Lancaster
technical associate: Jean Lewis
editorial writer: Susan McManus Johnson
art category manager: Lora Puls
lead graphic artist: Amy Temple
graphic artists: Jacob Casleton and Janie Wright
imaging technicians: Brian Hall, Stephanie Johnson, and Mark R. Potter
photography director: Katherine Laughlin
contributing photographer: Ken West
contributing photostylist: Sondra Daniel
publishing systems administrator: Becky Riddle
publishing systems assistants: Clint Hanson and John Rose

business staff

vice president and chief operations officer: Tom Siebenmorgen
director of finance and administration: Laticia Mull Dittrich
vice president, sales and marketing: Pam Stebbins
national accounts director: Martha Adams
sales and services director: Margaret Reinold
information technology director: Hermine Linz
controller: Francis Caple
vice president, operations: Jim Dittrich
comptroller, operations: Rob Thieme
retail customer service manager: Stan Raynor
print production manager: Fred F. Pruss

Library of Congress Catalog Number 2009939167
ISBN-13: 978-1-60140-465-7
ISBN-10: 1-60140-465-4

contents

nine-patch chain quilt

If you look closely at this quilt, you'll see that the grid pattern is actually formed with small nine-patch blocks. This antique quilt is simple to re-create by assembling the strip-pieced blocks and solid squares into long rows. The rows are stitched together and finished off with a squared border and basic grid quilting. So simple, so lovely!

FINISHED BLOCK SIZE: $2^5/8$" x $2^5/8$" (7 cm x 7 cm)
FINISHED QUILT SIZE: $75^1/2$" x $75^1/2$" (192 cm x 192 cm)

yardage requirements

*Yardage is based on 43"/44"
(109 cm/112 cm) wide fabric with
a usable width of 40" (102 cm).*

$4^7/8$ yds (4.5 m)
of blue print fabric

7 yds (6.4 m)
of white solid fabric

7 yds (6.4 m)
of fabric for backing

1 yd (91 cm)
of fabric for binding

$83^1/2$" x $83^1/2$"
(212 cm x 212 cm)
piece of batting

cutting the pieces

*Follow **Rotary Cutting**, page 85, to cut fabric. Cut all strips across the selvage-to-selvage width of the fabric unless otherwise indicated. All measurements include $^1/4$" seam allowances.*

from blue print fabric:
- Cut 63 **strips** $1^3/8$" wide.
- Cut 2 *lengthwise* **top/bottom inner borders** $1^1/2$" x 79".
- Cut 2 *lengthwise* **side inner borders** $1^1/2$" x 75".

from white solid fabric:
- Cut 27 strips $3^1/8$" wide. From these strips, cut 324 **setting squares** $3^1/8$" x $3^1/8$".
- Cut 51 **strips** $1^3/8$"w.
- Cut 2 *lengthwise* **top/bottom outer borders** $1^1/2$" x 79".
- Cut 2 *lengthwise* **side outer borders** $1^1/2$" x 75".
- From remaining width, cut 3 strips 5" wide. From these strips, cut 18 squares 5" x 5". Cut squares twice diagonally to make 72 **side setting triangles**.
- Cut 2 squares $2^3/4$" x $2^3/4$". Cut squares once diagonally to make 4 **corner setting triangles**.

assembling the quilt top

*Follow **Machine Piecing**, page 86, and **Pressing**, page 87. Use a ¹/₄" seam allowance unless otherwise stated.*

1. Assemble **strips** to make **Strip Set A**. Make 25 **Strip Set A's**. Cut across **Strip Set A's** at 1³/₈" intervals to make 722 **Unit 1's**.

Strip Set A
(make 25)

Unit 1
(make 722)

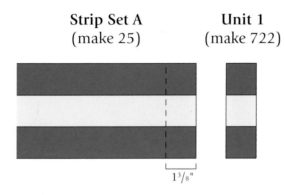

1³/₈"

2. Assemble **strips** to make **Strip Set B**. Make 13 **Strip Set B's**. Cut across **Strip Set B's** at 1³/₈" intervals to make 361 **Unit 2's**.

Strip Set B
(make 13)

Unit 2
(make 361)

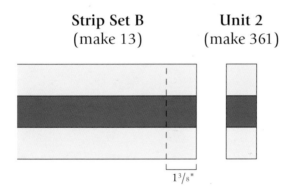

1³/₈"

3. Assemble 2 **Unit 1's** and 1 **Unit 2** to make **Block**. Make 361 **Blocks**.

Block (make 361)

4. Refer to **Assembly Diagram** to assemble **corner setting triangles**, **Blocks**, **side setting triangles**, and **setting squares** together into diagonal rows. Sew rows together to make center section of quilt top.

5. Assemble **borders** to make **Border Unit**. Make 2 **Side Border Units** and 2 **Top/Bottom Border Units**.

Border Units (make 4)

6. Referring to **Quilt Top Diagram**, page 9, follow **Adding Squared Borders**, page 87, to attach **Side**, then **Top** and **Bottom Border Units** to center section to complete **Quilt Top**. Round off corners as shown.

completing the quilt

1. Follow **Quilting**, page 88, to mark, layer, and quilt using **Quilting Diagram**, page 8, as a suggestion. Our quilt is hand quilted.

2. Cut a 30" square of binding fabric. Follow **Making Continuous Bias Strip Binding**, page 93, to make $2^{1}/_{2}$"w bias binding.

3. Follow Steps 1 and 2 of **Attaching Binding with Mitered Corners**, page 94, to pin binding to front of quilt. Easing binding around curves, sew binding to quilt. Fold binding over to quilt backing; blindstitch in place.

Assembly Diagram

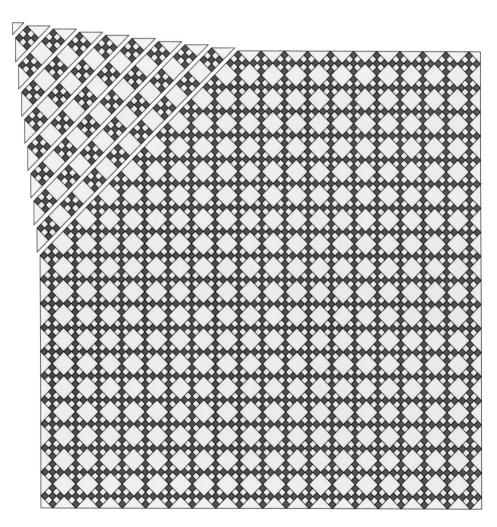

Quilting Diagram

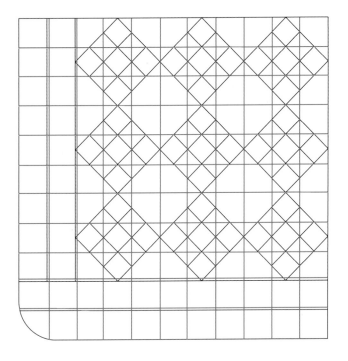

handling a large quilt
⎯when machine quilting⎯

The most difficult problems encountered when machine quilting often don't involve the actual quilting, but handling the bulk of a large quilt. You may want to try the following methods for managing the task.

- Use a work surface large enough to accommodate the quilt. If necessary, use a folding table, an adjustable-height ironing board, or other portable table to extend your work surface to the left of and behind your sewing machine. The entire weight of the quilt must be supported to prevent it from pulling the area under the needle, which could cause distortion of your quilting stitches.

- When possible, keep the largest portion of the quilt to your left. Always begin quilting in the center and work toward the outside of the quilt to minimize the amount of quilt under the head of the sewing machine.

- Try different methods of holding the portion of the quilt that must pass under the head of the machine. Some quilters simply accordion-fold the quilt, letting it fan out behind the machine. Or, you may wish to roll up the quilt and use one of the many devices on the market for holding the roll in place. Round and oval bicycle clips or plastic clips made specifically for quilters are available. The rolled quilt may also be pinned with large safety pins.

Quilt Top Diagram

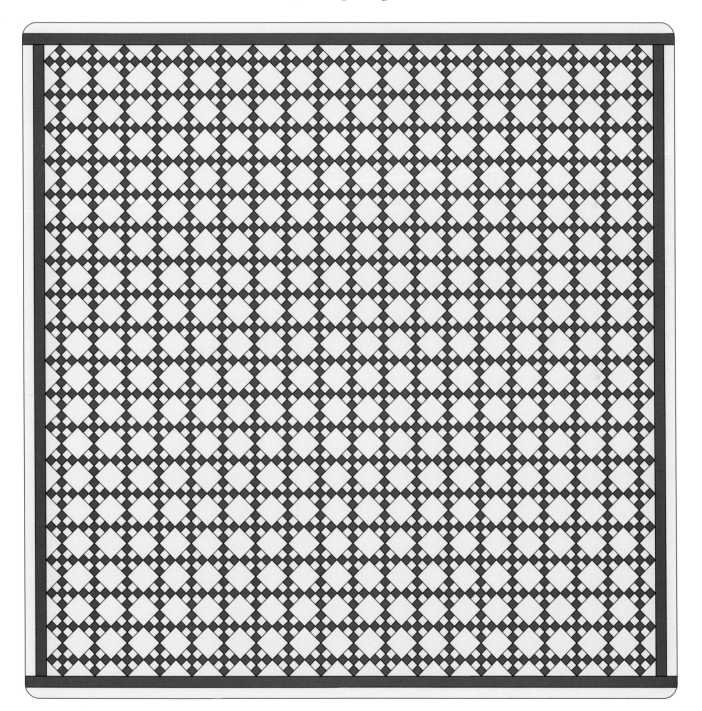

crown of thorns quilt

The Crown of Thorns block is pieced of squares and triangle-squares. The pieced blocks of this quilt are quilted in-the-ditch, meaning the quilting runs along the seams. However, the white setting squares and borders are quilted with flowers and leaves. If you find the idea of quilting curved lines to be daunting, try quilting the white spaces with a grid of straight lines.

FINISHED BLOCK SIZE: 10" x 10" (25 cm x 25 cm)
FINISHED QUILT SIZE: 76" x 76" (193 cm x 193 cm)

yardage requirements

Yardage is based on 43"/44" (109 cm/112 cm) wide fabric with a usable width of 40" (102 cm).

$5^3/_4$ yds (5.3 m)
of white solid fabric

$1^1/_8$ yds (1 m)
of green solid fabric

1 yd (91 cm)
of red solid fabric

$^1/_4$ yd (23 cm)
of yellow solid fabric

7 yds (6.4 m)
of fabric for backing

1 yd (91 cm)
of fabric for binding

84" x 84"
(213 cm x 213 cm)
piece of batting

cutting the pieces

*Follow **Rotary Cutting**, page 85, to cut fabric. Cut all strips across the selvage-to-selvage width of the fabric unless otherwise indicated. All measurements include $^1/_4$" seam allowances.*

From white solid fabric:
- Cut 7 **strips** $2^1/_2$"w.
- Cut 9 strips $10^1/_2$"w. From these strips, cut a total of 25 **setting squares** $10^1/_2$" x $10^1/_2$".
- Cut 4 *lengthwise* **border strips** 3" x 80".
- From remaining width, cut 22 strips 3"w. From these strips, cut 192 **squares** 3" x 3".

From green solid fabric:
- Cut 12 strips 3"w. From these strips, cut 144 **squares** 3" x 3".

From red solid fabric:
- Cut 7 **strips** $2^1/_2$"w.
- Cut 4 strips 3"w. From these strips, cut 48 **squares** 3" x 3".

From yellow solid fabric:
- Cut 2 **strips** $2^1/_2$"w.

assembling the quilt top

*Follow **Machine Piecing**, page 86, and **Pressing**, page 87. Use a $^1/_4$" seam allowance.*

1. Draw a diagonal line on wrong side of each white solid **square**.
2. With right sides together, place 1 white solid square on top of 1 red solid **square**. Stitch seam $^1/_4$" from each side of drawn line (**Fig. 1**).

Fig. 1

3. Cut along drawn line and press seam allowances to darker fabric to make 2 **Triangle-Square A's**. Make 96 **Triangle-Square A's**. Trim each Triangle-Square A to $2^1/_2$" x $2^1/_2$".

Triangle-Square A (make 96)

4. With right sides together place 1 white solid square on top of 1 green solid **square**. Stitch seam $^1/_4$" from each side of drawn line (**Fig. 2**).

Fig. 2

5. Cut along drawn line and press seam allowances to darker fabric to make 2 **Triangle-Square B's**. Make 288 **Triangle-Square B's**. Trim each Triangle-Square B to $2^1/_2$" x $2^1/_2$".

Triangle-Square B (make 288)

6. Assemble 1 **triangle-square A** and 3 **triangle-square B's** as shown to make **Unit 1**. Make 96 **Unit 1's**.

Unit 1 (make 96)

7. Assemble 2¹/₂"w **strips** as shown to make **Strip Set A**. Make 3 **Strip Set A's**. Cut across **Strip Set A's** at 2¹/₂" intervals to make a total of 48 **Unit 2's**.

Strip Set A
(make 3)

Unit 2
(make 48)

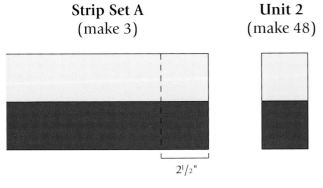

2¹/₂"

8. Assemble 2 **Unit 1's** and 1 **Unit 2** as shown to make **Unit 3**. Make 48 **Unit 3's**.

Unit 3 (make 48)

9. Assemble 2¹/₂"w **strips** as shown to make **Strip Set B**. Make 2 **Strip Set B's**. Cut across **Strip Set B's** at 2¹/₂" intervals to make a total of 24 **Unit 4's**.

Strip Set B
(make 2)

Unit 4
(make 24)

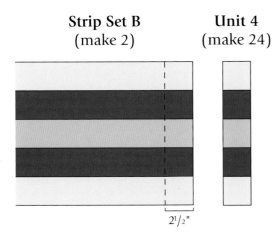

2¹/₂"

10. Assemble 2 **Unit 3's** and 1 **Unit 4** to make **Block**. Make 24 **Blocks**.

Block (make 24)

11. Assemble 4 **setting squares** and 3 **Blocks** as shown to make **Row A**. Make 4 **Row A's**.

Row A (make 4)

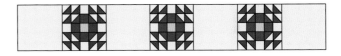

12. Assemble 4 **Blocks** and 3 **setting squares** as shown to make **Row B**. Make 3 **Row B's**.

Row B (make 3)

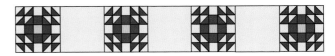

13. Referring to **Quilt Top Diagram**, assemble **Rows** to complete center section of quilt top.

14. Follow **Adding Mitered Borders**, page 88, and refer to **Quilt Top Diagram** to complete **Quilt Top**.

completing the quilt

1. Follow **Quilting**, page 88, to mark, layer, and quilt using **Quilting Diagram** as a suggestion. Use **Quilting Patterns**, pages 82-83, if desired.

2. Cut a 31" square of binding fabric. Follow **Making Continuous Bias Strip Binding**, page 93, to make $2^1/2$"w bias binding.

3. Follow **Attaching Binding with Mitered Corners**, page 94, to attach binding to quilt.

Quilting Diagram

Quilt Top Diagram

patriotic gem quilt

This red-white-and-blue quilt features a pieced block that has gathered many names over the years, although it is most often called "The Gem" or "Mosaic." It's very simple to assemble from squares, rectangles and triangles.

FINISHED BLOCK SIZE: 6" x 6" (15 cm x 15 cm)
FINISHED QUILT SIZE: 77" x 95" (196 cm x 241 cm)

Antique quilts are often too small to fit today's beds. Not only do our instructions include quick methods, but we've also resized our quilt to fit a full-size bed.

yardage requirements

Yardage is based on 43"/44" (109 cm/112 cm) wide fabric with a usable width of 40" (102 cm).

$3^7/_8$ yds (3.5 m) of blue print fabric

$4^1/_4$ yds (3.9 m) of red solid fabric

$2^1/_4$ yds (2.1 m) of white solid fabric

$7^1/_8$ yds (6.5 m) of fabric for backing

$^3/_4$ yd (69 cm) of fabric for binding

85" x 103" (216 cm x 262 cm) piece of batting

cutting the pieces

*Follow **Rotary Cutting**, page 85, to cut fabric. Cut all strips across the selvage-to-selvage width of the fabric unless otherwise indicated. All measurements include $^1/_4$" seam allowances.*

from blue print:
- Cut 8 **strips** $1^7/_8$" wide.
- Cut 9 strips $2^1/_2$"w. From these strips, cut 130 **squares** $2^1/_2$" x $2^1/_2$".
- Cut 2 *lengthwise* **top/bottom inner borders** $3^1/_2$" x $64^1/_2$".
- Cut 2 *lengthwise* **side inner borders** $3^1/_2$" x $88^1/_2$".
- From remaining fabric width, cut 26 crosswise strips $1^7/_8$"w. From these strips, cut 130 **small rectangles** $1^7/_8$" x $4^3/_4$".

from red solid:
- Cut 2 *lengthwise* **top/bottom outer borders** $5^1/_2$" x $70^1/_2$".
- Cut 2 *lengthwise* **side outer borders** $5^1/_2$" x $98^1/_2$".
- From remaining fabric, cut $6^1/_2$" wide strips. From these strips, cut 65 **setting squares** $6^1/_2$" x $6^1/_2$".

from white solid:
- Cut 4 **strips** 2" wide.
- Cut 17 strips $2^3/_8$" wide. From these strips, cut 260 squares $2^3/_8$" x $2^3/_8$". Cut squares once diagonally to make 520 **triangles**.
- Cut 9 strips $2^1/_2$"w. From these strips, cut 130 **squares** $2^1/_2$" x $2^1/_2$".

assembling the quilt top

*Follow **Machine Piecing**, page 86, and **Pressing**, page 87. Use a ¹/₄" seam allowance.*

1. Assemble **strips** to make **Strip Set**. Make 4 **Strip Sets**. Cut across **Strip Sets** at 2" intervals to make 65 **Unit 1's**.

Strip Set
(make 4)

Unit 1
(make 65)

2"

2. Assemble 2 **small rectangles** and 1 **Unit 1** to make **Unit 2**. Make 65 **Unit 2's**.

Unit 2 (make 65)

3. Draw a diagonal line on wrong side of each white solid **square**. With right sides together place 1 white solid square on top of 1 blue print **square**. Stitch seam ¹/₄" from each side of drawn line (**Fig. 1**).

Fig. 1

4. Cut along drawn line and press seam allowances to darker fabric to make 2 **Triangle-Squares**. Make 260 **Triangle-Squares**. Trim each Triangle-Square to 2" x 2".

Triangle-Squares (make 260)

5. Assemble 1 **triangle-square** and 2 **triangles** to make **Unit 3**. Make 260 **Unit 3's**.

Unit 3 (make 260)

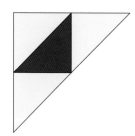

6. Assemble 4 **Unit 3's** and 1 **Unit 2** to make **Block**. Make 65 **Blocks**.

Block (make 65)

7. Assemble 5 **Blocks** and 5 **setting squares** to make **Row**. Make 13 **Rows**.

Row (make 13)

8. Referring to **Quilt Top Diagram**, page 20, assemble **Rows** to complete center section of quilt top.
9. Follow **Adding Squared Borders**, page 87, to attach **top**, **bottom**, and then **side inner borders** to center section of quilt top. Attach **top**, **bottom**, and then **side outer borders** to complete **Quilt Top**.

completing the quilt

1. Follow **Quilting**, page 88, to mark, layer, and quilt using **Quilting Diagram**, page 21, as a suggestion. Our quilt is hand quilted with outline quilting in the blocks, crosshatch quilting in the setting squares, and Baptist Fan designs on the borders.
2. Follow **Making Straight-Grain Binding**, page 93, to make 2^1/$_2$"w straight-grain binding.
3. Follow **Attaching Binding with Overlapped Corners**, page 96, to attach binding to quilt.

Quilt Top Diagram

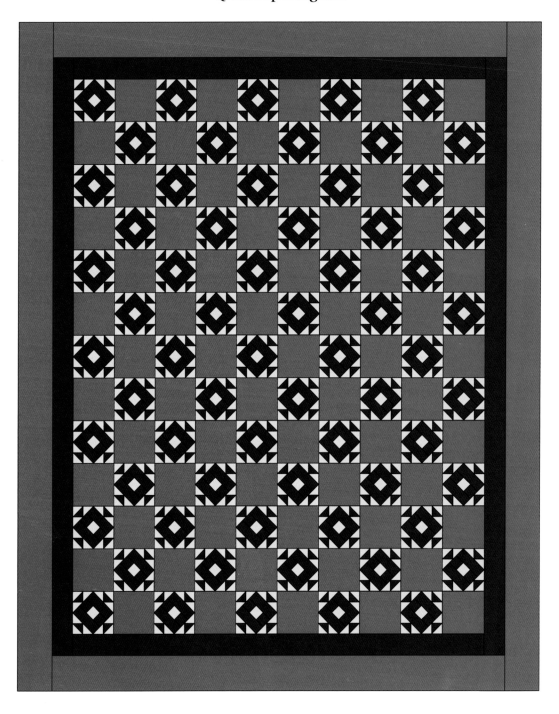

Quilting Diagram

— selecting the right batting —

Choosing the right batting will make your quilting job easier. Battings come in many different fibers and densities and give your quilt its personality and warmth.

- Bonded polyester batting is treated with a protective coating to stabilize the fibers and reduce "bearding," a process where bits of batting fibers work their way up through the quilt fabrics. It launders well with minimal to no shrinkage. Quilting at least every 3" to 4" is recommended.

  Choose low-loft batting for fine hand and machine quilting. It is lightweight, easy to quilt, and will give your completed project the "flat" appearance of a traditional quilt.

  Select extra-loft, high-loft, or fat batting when tying a quilt to give your project the puffy look of a comforter. Although these thicker battings can be hand quilted, you may not be satisfied with the end result.

- Cotton/Polyester batting may be machine or hand quilted. This batting must be quilted at least ever 3" to 4". It may not shrink as much as 100% cotton batting, but some shrinkage is still a possibility.

- Cotton batting may be machine or hand quilted, but must be quilted more closely than bonded or cotton/polyester batting for durability and to prevent shifting. Because of shrinkage that occurs during laundering, cotton batting gives your quilt the flat, wrinkled appearance similar to that of antique quilts. In fact, some manufacturers suggest prewashing the batting to help minimize shrinkage.

- Wool and Silk batting are generally more expensive. Bearding is a possibility with wool. There are also particular laundering specifications for each type of batting. Follow the manufacturer's instructions carefully if you decide to try one of these.

plaid quilt

Simple four-patch blocks and plain setting squares, all tied with embroidery floss for a quick finish—making a quilt just doesn't get easier than this! The cozy look of plaids and stripes will make this blanket a family favorite. It's a great pattern for when you're needing a gift in a hurry.

FINISHED BLOCK SIZE: $16^1/_2$" x $16^1/_2$" (42 cm x 42 cm)
FINISHED QUILT SIZE: $83^1/_2$" x 100" (212 cm x 254 cm)

yardage requirements

Yardage is based on 43"/44" (109 cm/112 cm) wide fabric with a usable width of 40" (102 cm).

$4^5/_8$ yds (4.2 m) **total**
of assorted dark plaids
(our quilt uses 11 different dark plaids)

$4^3/_8$ yds (4 m) **total**
of assorted light plaids and stripes
(our quilt uses 9 different light plaids and stripes)

$7^5/_8$ yds (7 m)
of fabric for backing

1 yd (91 cm)
of fabric for binding

$91^1/_2$" x 108" (232 cm x 274 cm)
piece of batting

You will also need:
Black embroidery floss

20 black 1" (25 mm) buttons

cutting the pieces

*Follow **Rotary Cutting**, page 85, to cut fabric. Cut all strips across the selvage-to-selvage width of the fabric. All measurements include $^1/_4$" seam allowances.*
from assorted dark plaids:
- Cut 46 **strips** $3^1/_4$"w.

from assorted light plaids and stripes:
- Cut 135 **squares** 6" x 6".

— using plaids and stripes —

Mixing lots of stripes and plaids in a single project is not as difficult as you might think when you keep the following guidelines in mind:

Think about plaids and stripes as you would any other fabric.
- Do your plaids and stripes fall into pleasing color families?
- Do you have a variety of scales in your fabrics? Are some plaids large-scale and some smaller scale? Is the same true for your striped fabrics?
- Will some of your fabrics "act like" background fabrics, while others may be bolder "feature fabrics?"

Cutting plaids and stripes doesn't have to be an ordeal either.
- If your plaids and stripes are woven, take care to align your cuts carefully with the grain of the fabric.
- If your fabrics are printed, consider aligning your cuts with the "visual grainline" — the straight lines of the design — even if the design doesn't match the true fabric grain.
- Or, you may ignore the "visual grainline" of printed fabrics altogether. Many of today's scrappy projects get their old-fashioned charm from plaids and stripes with designs that "veer off" the edges of the cut pieces.

assembling the quilt top

*Follow **Machine Piecing**, page 86, and **Pressing**, page 87. To achieve the scrappy look of our quilt, assemble strips, squares, and units in random fabric combinations. Use a ¹/₄" seam allowance.*

1. Assemble **strips** as shown to make **Strip Set A**. Make 23 **Strip Set A's**. Cut across **Strip Set A's** at 3¹/₄" intervals to make **Unit 1**. Make 270 **Unit 1's**.

Strip Set A (make 23)

3¹/₄"

Unit 1 (make 270)

2. Assemble 2 **Unit 1's** as shown to make **Unit 2**. Make 135 **Unit 2's**.

Unit 2 (make 135)

3. Assemble 2 **squares** and 1 **Unit 2** as shown to make **Unit 3**. Make 45 **Unit 3's**. Assemble 2 **Unit 2's** and 1 **square** as shown to make **Unit 4**. Make 45 **Unit 4's**.

Unit 3 (make 45)

Unit 4 (make 45)

4. Assemble 2 **Unit 3's** and 1 **Unit 4** as shown to make **Block A**. Make 15 **Block A's**. Assemble 2 **Unit 4's** and 1 **Unit 3** as shown to make **Block B**. Make 15 **Block B's**.

Block A (make 15)

Block B (make 15)

completing the quilt

1. Follow **Tying A Quilt**, page 92, to layer and tie quilt. Tie quilt at outside corners of **Unit 2's**. Before trimming floss ends, refer to **Assembly Diagram** to attach buttons to corners of **Blocks**.
2. Cut a 33" square of binding fabric. Follow **Making Continuous Bias Strip Binding**, page 93, to make 2^1/$_2$"w bias binding.
3. Follow **Attaching Binding with Overlapped Corners**, page 96, to attach binding to quilt.

5. Referring to **Assembly Diagram** and alternating **Blocks**, sew Blocks together into rows. Rotating rows as necessary, sew rows together to complete **Quilt Top**.

Assembly Diagram

ohio chain quilt

Another good name for this easy (and beautiful!) quilt would be "Chain of Stars." Originally known as the Variable Star, settlers on the American frontier renamed the Ohio Star block for the land where they homesteaded.

FINISHED BLOCK SIZE: 9" x 9" (23 cm x 23 cm)
FINISHED QUILT SIZE: 89" x 107" (226 cm x 272 cm)

yardage requirements

Yardage is based on 43"/44" (109 cm/112 cm) wide fabric with a usable width of 40" (102 cm).

9^1/$_8$ yds (8.3 m)
of cream solid fabric

2^3/$_4$ yds (2.5 m)
of navy print fabric
for inner borders

1 fat quarter [18" x 22"
(46 cm x 56 cm) piece] **each**
of 10 navy print and
10 red print fabrics

7^1/$_2$ yds (6.9 m)
of fabric for backing

1^1/$_8$ yds (1 m)
of fabric for binding

97" x 115"
(246 cm x 292 cm)
piece of batting

cutting the pieces

*Follow **Rotary Cutting**, page 85, to cut fabric. Cut all strips across the selvage-to-selvage width of the fabric unless otherwise indicated. All measurements include* ^{1}/$_4$" *seam allowances.*

from cream solid:
- Cut 30 strips 3^1/$_2$"w. From these strips, cut 320 **small squares** 3^1/$_2$" x 3^1/$_2$".
- Cut 20 strips 4^1/$_2$"w. From these strips, cut 160 **large squares** 4^1/$_2$" x 4^1/$_2$".
- Cut 2 *lengthwise* **side outer borders** 6^1/$_2$" x 110^1/$_2$".
- Cut 2 *lengthwise* **top/bottom outer borders** 6^1/$_2$" x 80^1/$_2$".

from navy print for inner borders:
- Cut 2 *lengthwise* **side inner borders** 2^1/$_2$" x 98^1/$_2$".
- Cut 2 *lengthwise* **top/bottom inner borders** 2^1/$_2$" x 76^1/$_2$".

from each navy print and red print fat quarter:
- Cut 8 **large squares** 4^1/$_2$" x 4^1/$_2$".
- Cut 4 **small squares** 3^1/$_2$" x 3^1/$_2$".

assembling the quilt top

*Follow **Machine Piecing**, page 86, and **Pressing**, page 87. Use matching print fabric when assembling each Hourglass Unit. Use a ¹/₄" seam allowance.*

1. Draw a diagonal line on wrong side of each cream **large square**. With right sides together place 1 cream **large square** on top of 1 navy **large square**. Stitch seam ¹/₄" from each side of drawn line (**Fig. 1**).

Fig. 1

2. Cut along drawn line and press seam allowances to darker fabric to make 2 **triangle-squares**. Use cream **large squares** and navy **large squares** to make 160 **triangle-squares**. Use cream **large squares** and red **large squares** to make 160 **triangle-squares**.

Triangle-Squares (make 320)

3. Referring to **Fig. 2**, place 2 matching **triangle-squares** right sides and opposite colors together, matching seams. Referring to **Fig. 3**, draw a diagonal line from corner to corner. Stitch ¹/₄" on both sides of drawn line. Cut apart on drawn line and press open to make 2 **hourglass units**. Repeat with remaining triangle-squares to make a total of 320 **hourglass units**. Trim each Hourglass Unit to 3¹/₂" x 3¹/₂".

Fig. 2

Fig. 3

Hourglass Unit (make 320)

4. Sew 2 cream **small squares** and 1 **hourglass unit** together to make **Unit 1**. Make 160 **Unit 1's**.

Unit 1 (make 160)

5. Sew 2 **hourglass units** and 1 navy **small square** together to make **Unit 2**. Make 80 **Unit 2's**.

Unit 2 (make 80)

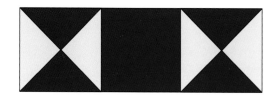

6. Sew 2 **Unit 1's** and 1 **Unit 2** together to make **Block**. Make 40 blue/white **Blocks** and 40 red/white **Blocks**.

Block (make 80)

7. Sew 8 **Blocks** together to make **Row**. Make 10 **Rows**.

Row (make 10)

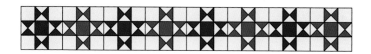

8. Referring to **Quilt Top Diagram** and rotating every other row, sew **Rows** together to make center section of quilt top.

9. Follow **Adding Squared Borders**, page 87, to sew **top**, **bottom**, then **side inner borders** to center section. Add **top**, **bottom**, and then **side outer borders** to complete **Quilt Top**.

completing the quilt

1. Follow **Quilting**, page 88, to mark, layer and quilt using **Quilting Diagram** as a suggestion. Our quilt is hand quilted.

2. Cut a 34" square of binding fabric. Follow **Making Continuous Bias Strip Binding**, page 93, to make $2^1/2$"w bias binding.

3. Follow **Attaching Binding With Mitered Corners**, page 94, to attach binding to quilt.

Quilting Diagram

Quilt Top Diagram

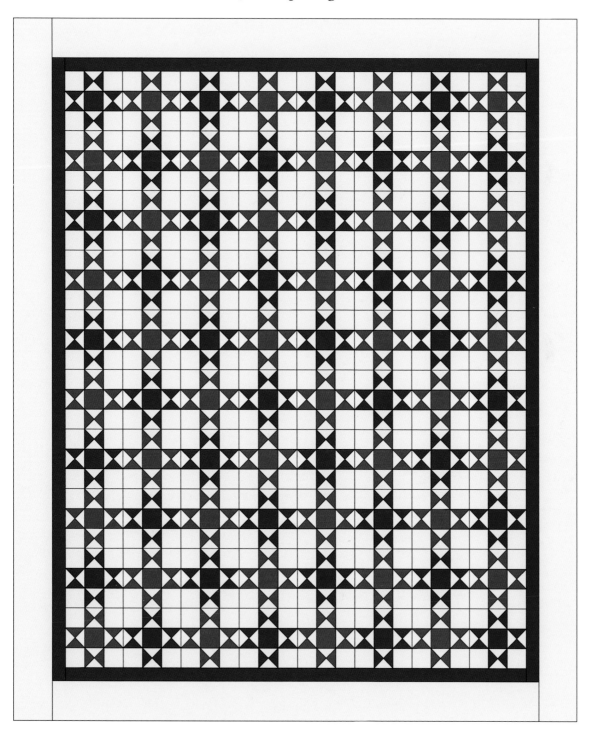

double nine-patch quilt

The blocks of the Double Nine-Patch are amazingly simple to piece, yet the pattern they create when set "on point" with plain setting squares seems complex. Because there are setting triangles on the ends of each row and on the four corners, this is also an excellent first quilt for learning how to cut and sew triangles. The border has mitered corners, a basic technique that creates a professional-looking finish.

FINISHED BLOCK SIZE: $11^1/4$" x $11^1/4$" (29 cm x 29 cm)
FINISHED QUILT SIZE: $75^3/4$" x $75^3/4$" (192 cm x 192 cm)

Our instructions eliminate bias edges and substitute a small red print for the checked fabric. The maker of our antique quilt dealt with many bias edges in order to match the direction of the checks in her quilt top.

yardage requirements
Yardage is based on 43"/44" (109 cm/112 cm) wide fabric with a usable width of 40" (102 cm).

5 yds (4.6 m)
of red print fabric

$3^3/8$ yds (3.1 m)
of navy print fabric

7 yds (6.4 m)
of fabric for backing

1 yd (91 cm)
of fabric for binding

84" x 84"
(213 cm x 213 cm)
piece of batting

cutting the pieces
*Follow **Rotary Cutting**, page 85, to cut fabric. Cut all strips across the selvage-to-selvage width of the fabric unless otherwise indicated. All measurements include $^1/4$" seam allowances.*

from red print:
- Cut 16 **strips** $1^3/4$" wide.
- Cut 8 strips $4^1/4$"w. From these strips, cut 64 **squares** $4^1/4$" x $4^1/4$".
- Cut 4 *lengthwise* **outer borders** $3^1/2$" x 80".
- From remaining fabric:
  - Cut 9 **setting squares** $11^3/4$" x $11^3/4$".
  - Cut 2 squares $8^7/8$" x $8^7/8$". Cut squares once diagonally to make 4 **corner setting triangles**.
  - Cut 3 squares $17^1/4$" x $17^1/4$". Cut each square twice diagonally to make 12 **side setting triangles**.

from navy print:
- Cut 20 **strips** $1^3/4$" wide.
- Cut 4 *lengthwise* **inner borders** 3" x 80".

assembling the quilt top

*Follow **Machine Piecing**, page 86, and **Pressing**, page 87. Use a $1/4$" seam allowance.*

1. Sew 2 navy **strips** and 1 red **strip** together to make **Strip Set A**. Make 8 **Strip Set A's**. Cut across **Strip Set A's** at $1^3/4$" intervals to make 160 **Unit 1's**.

Strip Set A   **Unit 1**
(make 8)   (make 160)

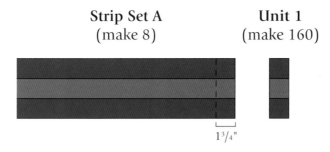

$1^3/4$"

2. Sew 2 red **strips** and 1 navy **strip** together to make **Strip Set B**. Make 4 **Strip Set B's**. Cut across **Strip Set B's** at $1^3/4$" intervals to make 80 **Unit 2's**.

Strip Set B   **Unit 2**
(make 4)   (make 80)

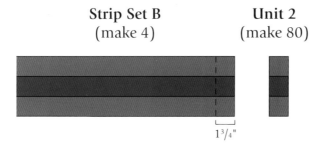

$1^3/4$"

3. Sew 2 **Unit 1's** and 1 **Unit 2** together to make **Unit 3**. Make 80 **Unit 3's**.

Unit 3 (make 80)

4. Sew 2 **Unit 3's** and 1 **square** together to make **Unit 4**. Make 32 **Unit 4's**.

Unit 4 (make 32)

5. Sew 2 **squares** and 1 **Unit 3** together to make **Unit 5**. Make 16 **Unit 5's**.

Unit 5 (make 16)

6. Sew 2 **Unit 4's** and 1 **Unit 5** together to make **Block**. Make 16 **Blocks**.

Block (make 16)

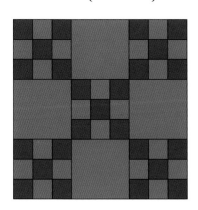

7. Referring to **Assembly Diagram**, page 36, sew **corner setting triangles**, **side setting triangles**, **Blocks**, and **setting squares** together into diagonal rows. Sew rows together to make center section of quilt top.

using precut ⎺quilting stencils⎺

Use a precut quilting stencil to make marking your quilt faster and easier. Plastic precut stencils are available at your favorite quilting store and come in a variety of classic designs. You'll probably find ones that closely match many of the quilting designs in this book. As an added bonus, the stencils are usually inexpensive and reusable!

8. Sew 1 **inner border** and 1 **outer border** together to make **Border Unit**. Make 4 **Border Units**.

Border Units (make 4)

9. Referring to **Quilt Top Diagram**, page 37, follow **Adding Mitered Borders**, page 88, to sew **Border Units** to center section to complete **Quilt Top**.

completing the quilt

1. Follow **Quilting**, page 88, to mark, layer, and quilt, using **Quilting Diagram**, page 36, as a suggestion. Our quilt is hand quilted.
2. Cut a 30" square of binding fabric. Follow **Making Continuous Bias Strip Binding**, page 93, to make 2¹/₂"w bias binding.
3. Follow **Attaching Binding With Mitered Corners**, page 94, to attach binding to quilt.

Quilting Diagram

Assembly Diagram

Quilt Top Diagram

old maid's puzzle quilt

This vintage quilt features alternating rows of Old Maid's Puzzle blocks and Hour Glass blocks. Other names for the larger block are Double X and Kindergarten. The simplicity of this quilt is played up by the use of only two fabrics. Navy and white are a classic combination.

FINISHED BLOCK SIZE: 9" x 9" (23 cm x 23 cm)
FINISHEDQUILT SIZE: $82^1/_2$" x 91" (210 cm x 231 cm)

yardage requirements

Yardage is based on 43"/44" (109 cm/112 cm) wide fabric with a usable width of 40" (102 cm).

$7^3/_8$ yds (6.7 m)
of white solid fabric

$2^3/_4$ yds (2.5 m)
of blue print fabric

$7^5/_8$ yds (7 m)
of fabric for backing

1 yd (91 cm)
of fabric for binding

$90^1/_2$" x 99"
(230 cm x 251 cm)
piece of batting

cutting the pieces

*Follow **Rotary Cutting**, page 85, to cut fabric. Cut all strips across the selvage-to-selvage width of the fabric unless otherwise indicated. All measurements include $^1/_4$" seam allowances.*

from white solid fabric:
- Cut 18 strips $4^3/_4$"w. From these strips, cut 72 **sashing strips** $4^3/_4$" x $9^1/_2$".
- Cut 10 strips $3^1/_2$"w. From these strips, cut 108 **medium squares** $3^1/_2$" x $3^1/_2$".
- Cut 11 strips 2"w. From these strips, cut 110 **small rectangles** 2" x $3^1/_2$".
- Cut 3 strips $5^3/_4$"w. From these strips, cut 18 **largest squares** $5^3/_4$" x $5^3/_4$".
- Cut 2 *lengthwise* **side inner borders** $1^7/_8$" x $87^1/_2$".
- Cut 2 *lengthwise* **top/bottom inner borders** $2^1/_8$" x $75^3/_4$".
- From remaining fabric:
  - Cut 14 strips 4"w. From these strips, cut 108 **large squares** 4" x 4".
  - Cut 2 **small squares** $2^1/_2$" x $2^1/_2$".

from blue print fabric:
- Cut 12 strips 2"w. From these strips, cut 220 **smallest squares** 2" x 2".
- Cut 11 strips 4"w. From these strips, cut 108 **large squares** 4" x 4".
- Cut 3 strips $5^3/_4$"w. From these strips, cut 18 **largest squares** $5^3/_4$" x $5^3/_4$".
- Cut 2 **small squares** $2^1/_2$" x $2^1/_2$".

assembling the quilt top

*Follow **Machine Piecing**, page 86, and **Pressing**, page 87. Use a ¹/₄" seam allowance.*

1. Draw a diagonal line on wrong side of each white solid **large square**. With right sides together place 1 white solid large square on top of 1 blue print **large square**. Stitch seam ¹/₄" from each side of drawn line (**Fig. 1**).

Fig. 1

2. Cut along drawn line and press seam allowances to darker fabric to make 2 **medium triangle-squares**. Make 216 **medium triangle-squares**. Trim each medium triangle-square to 3¹/₂" x 3¹/₂".

Medium Triangle-Squares (make 216)

3. Sew 1 **medium square** and 2 **medium triangle-squares** together to make **Unit 1**. Make 72 **Unit 1's**.

Unit 1 (make 72)

4. Sew 2 **medium triangle-squares** and 1 **medium square** together to make **Unit 2**. Make 36 **Unit 2's**.

Unit 2 (make 36)

5. Sew 2 **Unit 1's** and 1 **Unit 2** together to make **Block**. Make 36 **Blocks**.

Block (make 36)

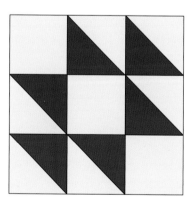

6. Draw a diagonal line on wrong side of each white solid **largest square**. With right sides together place 1 white solid **largest square** on top of 1 blue print **largest square**. Stitch seam ¹/₄" from each side of drawn line (**Fig. 2**).

Fig. 3

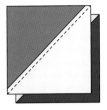

Fig. 2

7. Cut along drawn line and press seam allowances to darker fabric to make 2 **large triangle-squares**. Make 36 **large triangle-squares**.

Fig. 4

Sashing Block (make 36)

Large Triangle-Squares (make 36)

8. Place 2 **large triangle-squares** right sides and opposite colors together, matching seams (**Fig. 3**). Referring to **Fig. 4**, draw a diagonal line from corner to corner. Stitch ¹/₄" on both sides of marked line. Cut on marked line and press open to make 2 **Sashing Blocks**. Repeat with remaining **large triangle-squares** to make 36 **Sashing Blocks** (you will need 35 and have 1 left over). Trim each Sashing Block to 4³/₄" x 4³/₄".

9. Sew 6 **Blocks** and 5 **sashing strips** together to make **Row**. Make 6 **Rows**.

Row (make 6)

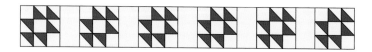

10. Sew 6 **sashing strips** and 5 **Sashing Blocks** together to make **Sashing Row**. Make 7 **Sashing Rows**.

Sashing Row (make 7)

11. Referring to **Quilt Top Diagram**, page 45, sew **Sashing Rows** and **Rows** together to make center section of quilt top.
12. Sew **top**, **bottom**, then **side inner borders** to center section.
13. Place 1 **smallest square** on 1 **small rectangle** and stitch diagonally (**Fig. 5**). Trim ¹/₄" from stitching (**Fig. 6**) and press open, pressing seam allowance toward darker fabric. Repeat for remaining **small rectangles**.

Fig. 5

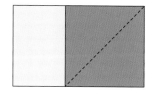

Fig. 6

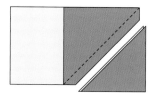

14. Place 1 **smallest square** on opposite end of 1 **small rectangle** and stitch diagonally (**Fig. 7**). Trim ¹/₄" from stitching (**Fig. 8**) and press open, pressing seam allowance toward darker fabric to make **Border Unit**. Repeat to make 112 **Border Units**.

Fig. 7

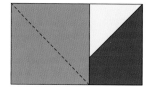

Fig. 8

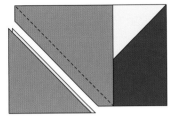

Border Unit (make 110)

15. Sew 26 **Border Units** together to make **Top Pieced Border**. Repeat to make **Bottom Pieced Border**.

Top/Bottom Pieced Border (make 2)

16. Sew 29 **Border Units** together to make **Side Pieced Border**. Make 2 **Side Pieced Borders**.

Side Pieced Border (make 2)

17. Follow Steps 1-2, page 40, using white solid **small squares** and blue print **small squares** to make 4 **Small Triangle-Squares**.
18. Sew 1 **small triangle-square** to each end of each **side pieced border**.
19. Referring to **Quilt Top Diagram**, page 45, sew **Top** and **Bottom Pieced Borders**, then **Side Pieced Borders** to center section to complete **Quilt Top**.

— "aging" new quilts —

Part of the charm of old quilts is their wrinkled appearance and time-softened colors, not to mention the lovely prints that can bring back memories of our grandmothers. You can re-create that nostalgic look in the quick-method quilts you make today by using one or all of the following suggestions.

- Use new fabrics that look like old fabrics! The reproduction prints that many fabric companies now carry have brought back some of the best colors and prints from the 1920's, 1930's, and even some from the 1800's!
- The wrong sides of some printed fabrics resemble faded, worn versions of the right sides of the fabrics. Using the wrong side of a fabric exclusively or mixing it with the right side of the print can lend a soft look to your quilt.
- Several types of batting, especially those that are all-cotton, shrink when washed. A gentle washing after quilting may help slightly shrink the batting and give your quilt that wrinkled, antique look.
- Scrap quilts often look old even if they are brand-new. Instead of using a planned fabric scheme, substitute scraps, just like the quilters of yesteryear did.
- Give your fabrics instant "age" by tea dyeing. Make a tea-dye bath using 3 to 4 regular tea bags per quart of hot tap water. Let the tea bags steep for 15 minutes before removing. Soak prewashed fabrics in the tea for 15 to 30 minutes, depending on the degree of "aging" you wish. Rinse well with cool water, squeeze, and iron dry.
- Commercial dyes are available to give new fabric an antique look. Check with your local quilt shop or fabric store for these supplies.

completing the quilt

1. Follow **Quilting**, page 88, to mark, layer, and quilt using **Quilting Diagram** as a suggestion. Our quilt is hand quilted.

2. Cut a 32" square of binding fabric. Follow **Making Continuous Bias Strip Binding**, page 93, to make $2^1/2$"w bias binding.

3. Follow **Attaching Binding With Mitered Corners**, page 94, to attach binding to quilt.

Quilting Diagram

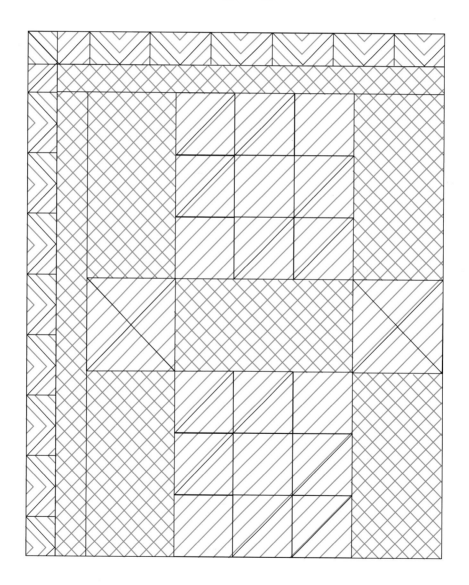

Quilt Top Diagram

friendship album quilt

Most historical sources tell us that album quilts were originally created for future brides by their friends. Album quilts usually include patches of light-color fabrics for signing with ink or embroidery. The Friendship Album blocks in this quilt are simplicity itself, just rectangles and squares to sew together. Today, a Friendship Album quilt would also make a great gift for a student going away to college.

FINISHED BLOCK SIZE: $12^1/_2$" x $12^1/_2$" (32 cm x 32 cm)
FINISHED QUILT SIZE: $73^1/_2$" x $90^1/_2$" (187 cm x 230 cm)

yardage requirements

Yardage is based on 43"/44" (109 cm/112 cm) wide fabric with a usable width of 40" (102 cm).

$2^5/_8$ yds (2.4 m)
of blue print fabric

$^5/_8$ yd (57 cm)
of blue check fabric

$^1/_8$ yd (11 cm) **each**
of 20 light print fabrics

$^1/_8$ yd (11 cm) **each**
of 20 dark print fabrics

$6^7/_8$ yds (6.3 m)
of fabric for backing

1 yd (91 cm)
of fabric for binding

$81^1/_2$" x $98^1/_2$"
(207 cm x 250 cm)
piece of batting

cutting the pieces

*Follow **Rotary Cutting**, page 85, to cut fabric. Cut all strips across the selvage-to-selvage width of the fabric. All measurements include $^1/_4$" seam allowances.*

from blue print fabric:
- Cut 17 strips 5"w. From these strips, cut 49 **sashing strips** 5" x 13".

from blue check fabric:
- Cut 4 strips 5"w. From these strips, cut 30 **sashing squares** 5" x 5".

from each light print fabric:
- Cut 1 strip 3"w. From this strip, cut 10 **squares** 3" x 3".
- Cut 1 **rectangle** 3" x 8".

from each dark print fabric:
- Cut 1 strip 3"w. From this strip, cut 12 **squares** 3" x 3".

assembling the quilt top

*Follow **Machine Piecing**, page 86, and **Pressing**, page 87. Use a ¹/₄" seam allowance.*

1. Referring to **Block Diagram**, sew 1 light **rectangle**, 10 light, and 12 dark **squares** together to make **Block**. Make 20 **Blocks**.

Block (make 20)

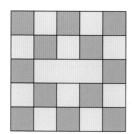

2. Referring to **Row Diagram**, sew 4 **Blocks** and 5 **sashing strips** together to make **Row**. Make 5 **Rows**.

Row (make 5)

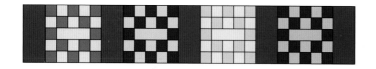

3. Referring to **Sashing Row Diagram**, sew 5 **sashing squares** and 4 **sashing strips** together to make **Sashing Row**. Make 6 **Sashing Rows**.

Sashing Row (make 6)

4. Referring to **Quilt Top Diagram**, sew **Rows** and **Sashing Rows** together to complete **Quilt Top**.

completing the quilt

1. Follow **Quilting**, page 88, to mark, layer, and quilt as desired. Our quilt is machine quilted with a flower in the blocks, an "X" in the sashing squares, and parallel lines in the sashings.
2. Cut a 31" square of binding fabric. Follow **Making Continuous Bias Strip Binding**, page 93, to make 2¹/₂"w bias binding.
3. Follow **Attaching Binding With Mitered Corners**, page 94, to attach binding to quilt.

Quilt Top Diagram

sailboat baby quilt

Quilted "waves" keep a flotilla of sailboats afloat on this sweet little blanket. The boats are composed of triangle-squares and rectangles for quick piecing. To ensure that your handiwork is long-wearing and destined to become an heirloom, the double-fold binding provides an extra layer of fabric along the edges of the quilt.

FINISHED BLOCK SIZE: 10" x 10" (25 cm x 25 cm)
FINISHED QUILT SIZE: 47" x 72" (119 cm x 183 cm)

To bring our vintage 1960's Sailboat quilt more in line with today's quick methods and standards, our instructions include simplified piecing and more durable double-fold binding.

yardage requirements

Yardage is based on 43"/44" (109 cm/112 cm) wide fabric with a usable width of 40" (102 cm).

$2^5/_8$ yds (2.4 m)
of blue solid fabric

$1^1/_2$ yds (1.4 m)
of white solid fabric

$4^1/_2$ yds (4.1 m)
of fabric for backing

$^7/_8$ yd (80 cm)
of fabric for binding

55" x 80"
(140 cm x 203 cm)
piece of batting

cutting the pieces

*Follow **Rotary Cutting**, page 85, to cut fabric. Cut all strips across the selvage-to-selvage width of the fabric unless otherwise indicated. All measurements include $^1/_4$" seam allowances.*
from blue solid fabric:
- Cut 5 strips $3^1/_2$"w. From these strips, cut 45 **squares** $3^1/_2$" x $3^1/_2$".
- Cut 2 *lengthwise* **side borders** 5" x $71^1/_2$".
- Cut 2 *lengthwise* **sashing strips** 4" x $71^1/_2$".
- From remaining fabric width, cut 4 strips 3"w. From these strips, cut 15 **rectangles** 3" x $5^1/_2$".
- From remaining fabric width, cut 9 strips 4" wide. From these strips, cut 18 **sashing rectangles** 4" x $10^1/_2$".
from white solid fabric:
- Cut 5 strips $3^1/_2$"w. From these strips, cut 45 **squares** $3^1/_2$" x $3^1/_2$".
- Cut 5 strips 3"w. From these strips, cut 30 **rectangles** 3" x $5^1/_2$".
- Cut 5 strips 3" wide. From these strips, cut 15 **large rectangles** 3" x $10^1/_2$".

sailboat baby quilt — 51

assembling the quilt top

*Follow **Machine Piecing**, page 86, and **Pressing**, page 87. Use a ¹/₄" seam allowance.*

1. Draw a diagonal line on wrong side of each white solid **square**. With right sides together place 1 white solid square on top of 1 blue solid **square**. Stitch seam ¹/₄" from each side of drawn line (**Fig. 1**).

Fig. 1

2. Cut along drawn line and press seam allowances to darker fabric to make 2 **Triangle-Squares**. Make 90 **Triangle-Squares**. Trim each Triangle-Square to 3" x 3".

Triangle-Squares (make 90)

3. Sew 4 **triangle-squares** together to make **Unit 1**. Make 15 **Unit 1's**.

Unit 1 (make 15)

4. Sew 1 **Unit 1** and 2 white solid **rectangles** together to make **Unit 2**. Make 15 Unit 2's.

Unit 2 (make 15)

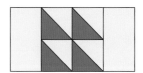

5. Sew 2 **triangle-squares** and 1 blue solid **rectangle** together to make **Unit 3**. Make 15 **Unit 3's**.

Unit 3 (make 15)

6. Sew 1 **Unit 2**, 1 **Unit 3**, and 1 **large rectangle** together to make **Block**. Make 15 **Blocks**.

Block (make 15)

7. Sew 6 **sashing rectangles** and 5 **Blocks** together to make 1 vertical **Row**. Make 3 **Rows**.

Row (make 3)

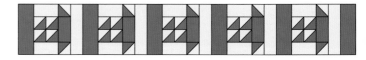

8. Referring to **Quilt Top Diagram**, sew 3 **Rows** and 2 **sashing strips** together to make center section of quilt top.

9. Sew **side borders** to center section to complete **Quilt Top**.

completing the quilt

1. Follow **Quilting**, page 88, to mark, layer, and quilt, using **Quilting Diagram** as a suggestion. Our quilt is hand quilted.
2. Cut a 27" square of binding fabric. Follow **Making Continuous Bias Strip Binding**, page 93, to make 2¹/₂"w bias binding.
3. Follow **Attaching Binding With Mitered Corners**, page 94, to attach binding to quilt.

Quilting Diagram

Quilt Top Diagram

— keeping a quilt journal —

Because of their beauty and durability, quilts are often handed down from one generation to the next. Unfortunately, however, information about the quiltmaker is often lost. You can make sure that there will always be a record of your quilts by keeping a quilt journal.

Your journal can be as simple or as detailed as you'd like. In a notebook or photo album (or a combination of the two), you can assemble an entry for each quilt that might include:

- The name that you have given the quilt and the traditional name of the pattern used.
- The dates you began and completed the quilt.
- A photo of the quilt or even shots made while the quilt is in progress.
- The name of the recipient and occasion, if the quilt was made as a gift.
- Swatches of the fabrics used and any special notes about fiber content or care.
- Your notes or drawings made while designing and making the quilt.
- A narrative diary of your thoughts during the time the quilt is being made.

Whatever you choose to include, you will find the journal both useful and enjoyable as you refer back to it in the future.

log cabin lullaby quilt

These pretty pastels keep Baby cozy! The Log Cabin block is an all-time favorite with quilters, and the trim-as-you-go method reduces the worry of working with small fabric pieces. A quilting motif of hearts and flowers adds an extra touch of sweetness to the border.

FINISHED BLOCK SIZE: $5^3/_4$" x $5^3/_4$" (15 cm x 15 cm)
FINISHED QUILT SIZE: 38" x $49^1/_2$" (97 cm x 126 cm)

yardage requirements

Yardage is based on 43"/44" (109 cm/112 cm) wide fabric with a usable width of 40" (102 cm).

$1^1/_2$ yds (1.4 m)
of white solid fabric

$1/_2$ yd (46 cm)
of pink check fabric

$1/_4$ yd (23 cm)
of pink print fabric

$1/_4$ yd (23 cm) **each**
of yellow print, yellow check,
blue print, blue stripe, blue check,
purple print, purple check,
green print, green stripe,
and aqua print

$3^1/_4$ yds (3 m)
of fabric for backing

46" x $57^1/_2$"
(117 cm x 146 cm)
piece of batting

cutting the pieces

*Follow **Rotary Cutting**, page 85, to cut fabric. Cut all strips across the selvage-to-selvage width of the fabric. All measurements include $1/_4$" seam allowances.*

from white solid fabric:
- Cut 2 strips $1^3/_4$"w. From these strips, cut 24 **squares** $1^3/_4$" x $1^3/_4$".
- Cut 18 **strips** $1^1/_4$"w.
- Cut 2 **side outer borders** $5^1/_2$" x 39".
- Cut 2 **top/bottom outer borders** $5^1/_2$" x $27^1/_2$".

from pink check fabric:
- Cut 2 **side inner borders** $2^1/_2$" x 39".
- Cut 2 **top/bottom inner borders** $2^1/_2$" x $23^1/_2$".
- Cut 2 **strips** $1^1/_4$"w.

from pink print fabric:
- Cut 1 strip $5^1/_2$"w. From this strip, cut 4 **corner squares** $5^1/_2$" x $5^1/_2$".
- Cut 2 **strips** $1^1/_4$"w.

from yellow print, yellow check, blue print, blue stripe, blue check, purple print, purple check, green print, green stripe, and aqua print:
- Cut 2 **strips** $1^1/_4$"w from *each* fabric.

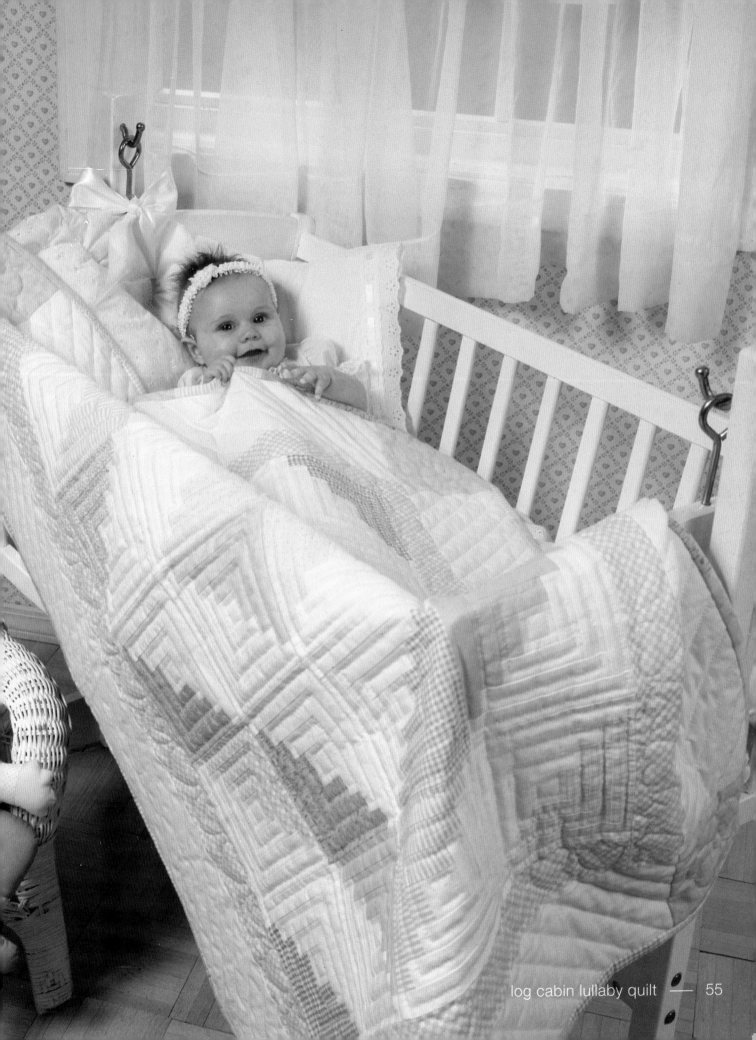

assembling the quilt top

*Follow **Machine Piecing**, page 86, and **Pressing**, page 87. Use a ¹/₄" seam allowance.*

1. Place 1 pink check **strip** on 1 **square** with right sides together and raw edges matching. Stitch as shown in **Fig. 1**. Trim strip even with square (**Fig. 2**); press open (**Fig. 3**).

Fig. 1

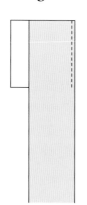

Fig. 2

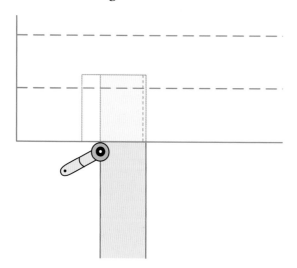

Fig. 3

2. Turn **square** ¹/₄ turn to the left and repeat Step 1 to add the next "log" as shown in **Figs. 4-6**.

Fig. 4

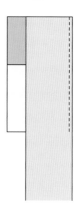

Fig. 5

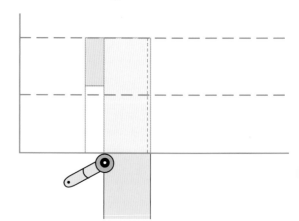

Fig. 6

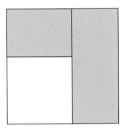

3. Repeat Step 2 to add **white** strips to remaining 2 sides of **square** (**Fig. 7**).

Fig. 7

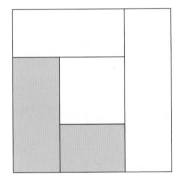

4. Continue adding **strips**, alternating 2 pink check strips and 2 white strips until there are 3 strips on each side of square to make **Block**. Make 2 **Blocks** using pink check and white strips.

Block

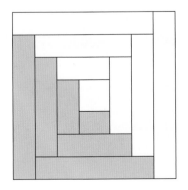

5. Using remaining strips, repeat Steps 1-4 to make a total of 24 **Blocks** (2 Blocks using *each* color print, check, or stripe).

6. Referring to **Quilt Top Diagram**, page 58, for color placement, sew **Blocks** together into rows. Sew rows together to make center section of quilt top.

7. Sew **top**, **bottom**, then **side inner borders** to center section.

8. Sew 1 **corner square** to each end of each **side outer border**. Sew **top**, **bottom**, then **side outer borders** to center section to complete **Quilt Top**.

completing the quilt

1. Follow **Quilting**, page 88, to mark, layer, and quilt, using **Quilting Diagram**, page 59, as a suggestion. Our quilt is hand quilted.

2. To make pieced binding, cut remaining scraps of print, check, and stripe fabrics into pieces $2^1/_2$"w and varying in length from $3^1/_2$" to $6^1/_2$". Sew pieces together along $2^1/_2$"w edges to make 2 **top/bottom binding pieces** 40"l and 2 **side binding pieces** 52"l. Follow **Attaching Binding with Overlapped Corners**, page 96, to bind quilt.

Quilt Top Diagram

Quilting Diagram

— organizing your quiltmaking —

Using our quick methods makes quiltmaking faster and easier, as well as more enjoyable and satisfying. Organizing your supplies and workspace will help you to accomplish even more during the time you have to devote to quiltmaking. Try the following suggestions:

- If you don't have a sewing room, use a portable, easily stored container to keep all your tools and supplies in one place. You can use laundry baskets that can be stacked in a closet, under-bed storage boxes, or even a cardboard box stored under a skirted table.

- Store all the materials for an individual project in a smaller box or other container. Include the fabric, thread, and other supplies, as well as the project instructions and any special tools or materials you may need. Label the individual project boxes.

- Before putting a project away, label any pieces that may be difficult to identify later. Make notes on the instructions (use self-stick notes if you don't want to write in your books) that will help you quickly pick up where you left off.

- Never put away a project when you're having a problem. Rip out mistakes and work out problems before you stop working so that you'll look forward to getting back to the project.

- Invest in tools and supplies that will make your work easier. Trying to work with poor-quality tools or the wrong tool for the job will only lead to frustration and dissatisfaction with the results.

- Choose projects carefully. Alternate quilts that challenge your time and abilities with simpler, smaller projects like wall hangings or lap quilts. Include fast, fun projects that you can finish quickly. The satisfaction of finishing one project is always good motivation to finish another.

butterfly at the crossroads quilt

Sometimes the use of just two fabric colors can produce a wonderfully vivid quilt. This red-and-black quilt was created with a traditional Butterfly at the Crossroads pattern, a block that features four pieced squares joined together by the long rectangles and small central square of the "cross." Because of its simple coloring, this quilt is also a good opportunity for showcasing a favorite quilting design.

FINISHED BLOCK SIZE: $11^1/_2$" x $11^1/_2$" (29 cm x 29 cm)
FINISHED QUILT SIZE: 66" x $75^1/_2$" (168 cm x 192 cm)

yardage requirements

Yardage is based on 43"/44" (109 cm/112 cm) wide fabric with a usable width of 40" (102 cm).

$4^1/_8$ yds (3.8 m)
of black solid fabric

3 yds (2.7 m)
of red solid fabric

$4^3/_4$ yds (4.3 m)
of fabric for backing

1 yd (91 cm)
of fabric for binding

74" x $83^1/_2$"
(188 cm x 212 cm)
piece of batting

cutting the pieces

*Follow **Rotary Cutting**, page 85, to cut fabric. Cut all strips across the selvage-to-selvage width of the fabric unless otherwise indicated. All measurements include $^1/_4$" seam allowances.*

from black solid:

- Cut 6 strips $2^1/_2$"w. From these strips, cut 16 **sashing strips** $2^1/_2$" x 12".
- Cut 12 strips 2"w. From these strips, cut 80 **rectangles** 2" x $5^1/_2$".
- Cut 7 strips 3"w. From these strips, cut 80 **small squares** 3" x 3".
- Cut 4 *lengthwise* **top/bottom borders** 2" x $69^1/_2$".
- Cut 4 *lengthwise* **side borders** 2" x 79".
- From remaining width, cut 14 strips $3^1/_2$"w. From these strips, cut 80 **squares** $3^1/_2$" x $3^1/_2$" for triangle-squares.

from red solid:

- Cut 1 strip 2"w. From this strip, cut 20 **center squares** 2" x 2".
- Cut 7 strips 3"w. From these strips, cut 80 **small squares** 3" x 3".
- Cut 2 *lengthwise* **top/bottom borders** 2" x $69^1/_2$".
- Cut 2 *lengthwise* **side borders** 2" x 79".
- Cut 5 *lengthwise* **sashing strips** $2^1/_2$" x 66".
- From remaining width, cut 16 strips $3^1/_2$"w. From these strips, cut 80 **squares** $3^1/_2$" x $3^1/_2$" for triangle-squares.

assembling the quilt top

*Follow **Machine Piecing**, page 86, and **Pressing**, page 87. Use a ¹/₄" seam allowance.*

1. Draw a diagonal line on wrong side of each red solid **square**. With right sides together place 1 red solid square on top of 1 black solid **square**. Stitch seam ¹/₄" from each side of drawn line (**Fig. 1**).

Fig. 1

2. Cut along drawn line and press seam allowances to darker fabric to make 2 **Triangle-Squares**. Make 160 **Triangle-Squares**. Trim each Triangle-Square to 3" x 3".

Triangle-Squares (make 160)

3. Assemble 1 black solid **small square** and 1 **triangle-square** as shown to make **Unit 1**. Make 80 **Unit 1's**.

Unit 1 (make 80)

4. Assemble 1 **triangle-square** and 1 red solid **small square** as shown to make **Unit 2**. Make 80 **Unit 2's**.

Unit 2 (make 80)

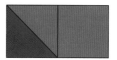

5. Assemble 1 **Unit 1** and 1 **Unit 2** as shown to make **Unit 3**. Make 80 **Unit 3's**.

Unit 3 (make 80)

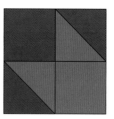

6. Assemble 2 **Unit 3's** and 1 **rectangle** as shown to make **Unit 4**. Make 40 **Unit 4's**.

Unit 4 (make 40)

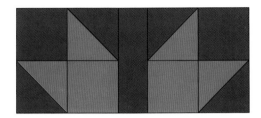

7. Assemble 2 **rectangles** and 1 **center square** as shown to make **Unit 5**. Make 20 **Unit 5's**.

Unit 5 (make 20)

8. Assemble 2 **Unit 4's** and 1 **Unit 5** as shown to make **Block**. Make 20 **Blocks**.

Block (make 20)

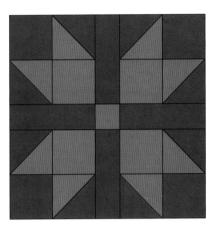

9. Assemble 5 **Blocks** and 4 black solid **sashing strips** as shown to make **Row**. Make 4 **Rows**.

Row (make 4)

10. Referring to **Quilt Top Diagram**, assemble **Rows** and **sashing strips** to complete center section of quilt top.
11. Assemble borders as shown to make **Border Units**. Make 2 **Top/Bottom Border Units** and 2 **Side Border Units**.

Border Unit

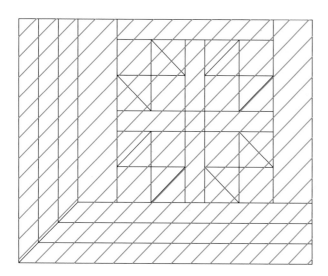

12. Follow **Adding Mitered Borders**, page 88, to attach **Border Units** to center section of quilt top to complete **Quilt Top**.

Quilting Diagram

completing the quilt

1. Follow **Quilting**, page 88, and **Quilting Diagram** to mark, layer, and quilt.
2. Cut a 30" square of binding fabric. Follow **Making Continuous Bias Strip Binding**, page 93, to make $2^1/2$"w bias binding.
3. Follow **Attaching Binding with Mitered Corners**, page 94, to attach binding to quilt.

— thrifty quilt backings —

Sometimes a quilt top will be just a bit too wide to use 2 lengths of 45"w fabric for the backing. Instead of buying another full length of fabric, you might want to try piecing a section of the backing using leftover fabrics from your quilt top.

1. Determine how much extra width you will need to fit your quilt top. Two lengths of 45"w fabric, after shrinkage and trimming the selvages, will be approximately 79"w when sewn together. If your quilt top is 80"w, your backing will need to measure at least 88"w, so you will need to add a 9"w section to your quilt backing.
2. Cut fabrics leftover from your quilt top into selvage-to selvage strips that vary from 1"w to 3"w.
3. Sew the strips together in random color order to form a strip set.
4. From the strip set, cut sections the width you need to add to your quilt backing, plus seam allowances.
5. Sew these sections together until they measure the length of your quilt backing. Leftover strips from your quilt top that are shorter than selvage-to-selvage width may be trimmed and added to the pieced section, if necessary.
6. Sew the new pieced section and your backing pieces together. The pieced section may be added in the center between the 2 lengths of backing fabric or along 1 edge. You may even wish to set this piece off-center by cutting 1 length of backing fabric lengthwise and sewing the pieced section between the 2 pieces.

Quilt Top Diagram

chinese coins quilt

The Amish communities of Indiana, Ohio, and Pennsylvania are renowned for the skill of their quilters. This lovely quilt was made by Amish craftswomen in Ohio. To create a similar quilt, rotary cut long strips of fabric, piece them into a rectangle, and cut the rectangle into columns that stack together for quick assembly. The black background unifies the wide variety of colors.

FINISHED QUILT SIZE: 68" x 81^1/$_2$" (173 cm x 207 cm)

yardage requirements

Yardage is based on 43"/44" (109 cm/112 cm) wide fabric with a usable width of 40" (102 cm).

4^1/$_8$ yds (3.8 m)
of black solid fabric

2 yds (1.8 m) **total**
of assorted solid fabrics
(40" [102 cm] wide strips
are required)

5 yds (4.6 m)
of fabric for backing

^{5}/$_8$ yd (57 m)
of fabric for binding

76" x 89^1/$_2$"
(193 cm x 227 cm)
piece of batting

cutting the pieces

*Follow **Rotary Cutting**, page 85, to cut fabric. Cut all strips across the selvage-to-selvage width of the fabric unless otherwise indicated. All measurements include ^{1}/$_4$" seam allowances.*

from black solid:

- Cut 2 *lengthwise* **side outer borders** 8" x 84^1/$_2$".
- Cut 2 *lengthwise* **top/bottom outer borders** 8" x 56^1/$_2$".
- Cut 5 *lengthwise* **sashing strips** 6" x 61^1/$_2$".

from assorted solid fabrics:

- Cut 1 or more **strips** from each fabric in widths varying from 1^1/$_2$"w to 2^1/$_4$"w.

assembling the quilt top

*Follow **Machine Piecing**, page 86, and **Pressing**, page 87. Assemble strips and units in random fabric combinations. Use a 1/4" seam allowance.*

1. Assemble **strips** as shown to make a **Strip Set** 21½"l. Make 3 **Strip Sets**. Cut across **Strip Sets** at 5½" intervals to make a total of 12 **Unit 1's**. Cut across remaining **Strip Sets** at 2¾" intervals to make a total of 11 **Unit 2's**.

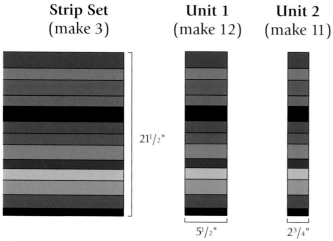

Strip Set (make 3)   **Unit 1** (make 12)   **Unit 2** (make 11)

21½"   5½"   2¾"

2. Sew short edges of all **Unit 1's** together to make 1 **Pieced Strip**. Cut across **Pieced Strip** at 61½" intervals to make a total of 4 **Unit 3's**.

Unit 3 (make 4)

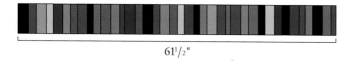

61½"

3. Referring to **Quilt Top Diagram**, assemble **Unit 3's** and **sashing strips** to complete center section of quilt top.

4. Sew short edges of all **Unit 2's** together to make 1 **Border Strip**. Cutting across **Border Strip**, cut 2 **top/bottom inner borders** 48" long. Cutting across remainder of **Border Strip** cut 2 **side inner borders** 66" long.

Border Strip (make 1)

5. Refer to **Quilt Top Diagram** and attach **top**, **bottom**, and then **side inner borders** to center section of quilt top. Follow **Adding Squared Borders**, page 87, to add **top**, **bottom**, and then **side outer borders** to complete **Quilt Top**.

completing the quilt

1. Follow **Quilting**, page 88, and **Quilting Diagram** to mark, layer, and quilt. If desired, use Cable Pattern, page 84. To mark border, cut a piece of paper the size of the border to be marked. Refer to the **Quilting Diagram**, to draw placement line on paper. Trace feather pattern, page 83, onto template plastic and cut out. Placing narrow point of template along placement line, use a marking pencil or pen to draw feathers, reversing template and adjusting spacing of feathers as necessary on curves and corners (**Figs. 1 - 2**). After pattern is drawn, follow **Marking Quilting Lines**, page 89, to mark borders.

Fig. 1

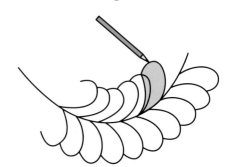

Fig. 2

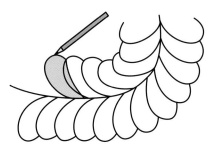

2. Follow **Making Straight-Grain Binding**, page 93, to make 2¹/₂"w straight-grain binding.
3. Follow **Attaching Binding with Overlapped Corners**, page 96, to attach binding to quilt.

Quilting Diagram

Quilt Top Diagram

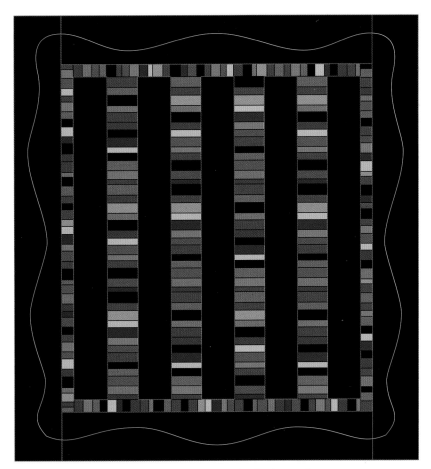

Blue line indicates placement line for feather quilting pattern.

roman stripe quilt

Known as Roman Stripe when pieced using print fabrics, this classic pattern is more commonly called Sunshine and Shadows among the Amish of the Midwest. Quilters in these communities traditionally use only solid fabrics for the stripes with black for the background. To create the striped sections, we rotary cut strip-pieced sets using a ruler that produces accurate angles. The fast and simple pattern is a perfect project for a first-time quilter.

FINISHED BLOCK SIZE: 7" x 7" (18 cm x 18 cm)
FINISHED QUILT SIZE: 78" x 92" (198 cm x 234 cm)

yardage requirements

Yardage is based on 43"/44" (109 cm/112 cm) wide fabric with a usable width of 40" (102 cm).

$4^3/_8$ yds (4 m)
of black plaid fabric

$2^3/_8$ yds (2.2 m) **total**
of assorted plaid fabrics

2 yds (1.8 m)
of red plaid fabric

$1^3/_4$ yds (1.6 m)
of black solid fabric

$7^1/_4$ yds (6.6 m)
of fabric for backing

1 yd (91 cm)
of fabric for binding

86" x 100"
(218 cm x 254 cm)
piece of batting

You will also need:
Companion Angle™ Rotary Cutting
Ruler (made by EZ International)

cutting the pieces

Follow Rotary Cutting, page 85, to cut fabric. Cut all strips across the selvage-to-selvage width of the fabric unless otherwise indicated. All measurements include $^1/_4$" seam allowances.

from black plaid fabric:
- Cut 2 *lengthwise* **top/bottom outer borders** $12^1/_4$" x $81^1/_2$".
- Cut 2 *lengthwise* **side outer borders** $12^1/_4$" x 72".

from assorted plaid fabrics:
- Cut a total of 44 **strips** $1^3/_4$" wide.

from red plaid fabric:
- Cut 2 *lengthwise* **top/bottom inner borders** $2^3/_4$" x 58".
- Cut 2 *lengthwise* **side inner borders** $2^3/_4$" x 72".

from black solid fabric:
- Cut 7 strips $7^7/_8$"w. From these strips, cut 32 squares $7^7/_8$" x $7^7/_8$". Cut squares once diagonally to make 64 **triangles** (you will need 63 and have 1 left over).

assembling the quilt top

*Follow **Machine Piecing**, page 86, and **Pressing**, page 87. Use a ¹/₄" seam allowance.*

1. Sew 4 **strips** together in random color order to make **Strip Set**. Make 11 Strip Sets.

Strip Set (make 11)

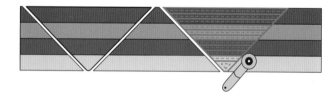

2. Aligning top and bottom edges of ruler with long edges of Strip Set, use Companion Angle ruler to cut 63 **Unit 1's** from **Strip Sets**, turning ruler 180° after each cut (**Fig. 1**).

Fig. 1

Unit 1 (make 63)

3. Sew 1 **Unit 1's** and 1 **triangle** together to make **Block**. Make 63 **Blocks**.

Block (make 63)

4. Sew 7 **Blocks** together to make **Row**. Make 9 **Rows**.

Row (make 9)

Quilting Diagram

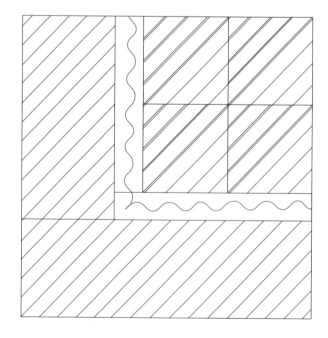

5. Referring to **Quilt Top Diagram**, sew **Rows** together to make center section of quilt top.

6. Follow **Adding Squared Borders**, page 87, to sew **side**, then **top** and **bottom inner borders** to center section. Add **side**, then **top** and **bottom outer borders** to complete **Quilt Top**.

completing the quilt

1. Follow **Quilting**, page 88, to mark, layer, and quilt, using **Quilting Diagram** as a suggestion. Our quilt is machine quilted.

2. Cut a 32" square of binding fabric. Follow **Making Continuous Bias Strip Binding**, page 93, to make 2^1/$_2$"w bias binding.

3. Follow **Attaching Binding With Mitered Corners**, page 94, to attach binding.

Quilt Top Diagram

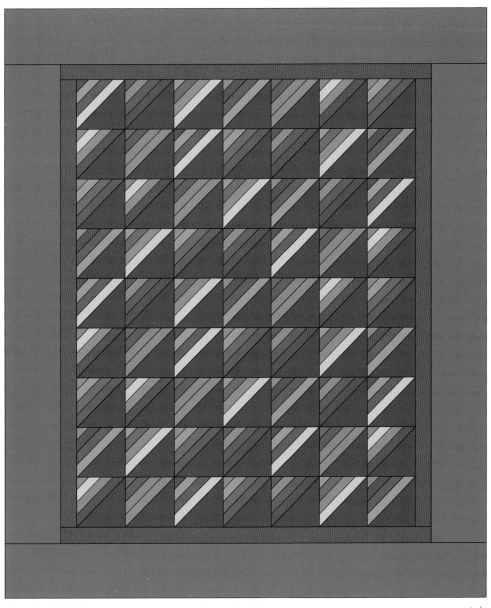

burgoyne surrounded quilt

This historical quilt pattern commemorates the Revolutionary War surrender of British General John Burgoyne during the battle at Saratoga in 1777. Burgoyne Surrounded quilts are usually depicted as a pattern of red on a white background, but the reversed colors also give a spectacular effect. Although it looks complex, the quilt is actually an assembly of sixteen large blocks, each of which is just a series of simple squares and rectangles.

FINISHED BLOCK SIZE: 22" x 22" (56 cm x 56 cm)
FINISHED QUILT SIZE: 89" x 89" (226 cm x 226 cm)

yardage requirements

Yardage is based on 43"/44" (109 cm/112 cm) wide fabric with a usable width of 40" (102 cm).

$2^3/_4$ yds (2.5 m)
of white solid fabric

$7^3/_4$ yds (7.1 m)
of red solid fabric

$8^1/_8$ yds (7.4 m)
of fabric for backing

$1^1/_8$ yds (1 m)
of fabric for binding

97" x 97"
(246 cm x 246 cm)
piece of batting

cutting the pieces

*Follow **Rotary Cutting**, page 85, to cut fabric. Cut all strips across the selvage-to-selvage width of the fabric. All measurements include $^1/_4$" seam allowances.*
from white solid fabric:
- Cut 34 **narrow strips** $1^1/_2$"w.
- Cut 12 **wide strips** 3"w.

from red solid fabric:
- Cut 31 **narrow strips** $1^1/_2$"w.
- Cut 8 **wide strips** 3"w.
- Cut 12 strips $2^1/_2$" w. From these strips, cut 128 **small rectangles** $2^1/_2$" x $3^1/_2$".
- Cut 43 strips $3^1/_2$" w. From these strips, cut 64 **large rectangles** $3^1/_2$" x $6^1/_2$" and 64 **border strips** $3^1/_2$" x $16^1/_2$".

assembling the quilt top

*Follow **Machine Piecing**, page 86, and **Pressing**, page 87. Use a ¼" seam allowance unless otherwise stated.*

1. Sew 2 white **wide strips** and 1 red **narrow strip** together to make **Strip Set A**. Make 3 **Strip Set A's**. Cut across Strip Set A's at 3" intervals to make 32 **Unit 1's**.

Strip Set A (make 3)   **Unit 1** (make 32)

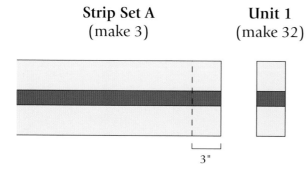

3"

2. Sew 2 white **wide strips** and 1 red **narrow strip** together to make **Strip Set B**. Make 3 **Strip Set B's**. Cut across Strip Set B's at 1½" intervals to make 64 **Unit 2's**.

Strip Set B (make 3)   **Unit 2** (make 64)

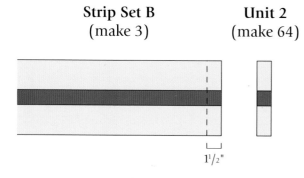

1½"

3. Sew 2 red **wide strips** and 1 white **narrow strip** together to make **Strip Set C**. Make 4 **Strip Set C's**. Cut across Strip Set C's at 1½" intervals to make 80 **Unit 3's**.

Strip Set C (make 4)   **Unit 3** (make 80)

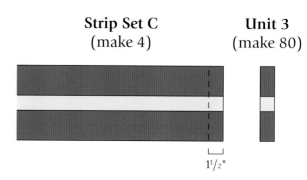

1½"

4. Sew 2 white **narrow strips** and 1 red **narrow strip** together to make **Strip Set D**. Make 10 **Strip Set D's**. Cut across Strip Set D's at 1½" intervals to make 256 **Unit 4's**.

Strip Set D (make 10)   **Unit 4** (make 256)

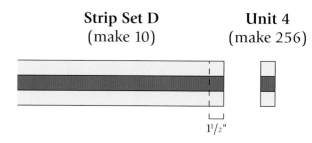

1½"

5. Sew 2 red **narrow strips** and 1 white **narrow strip** together to make **Strip Set E**. Make 5 **Strip Set E's**. Cut across Strip Set E's at 1½" intervals to make 128 **Unit 5's**.

Strip Set E (make 5)   **Unit 5** (make 128)

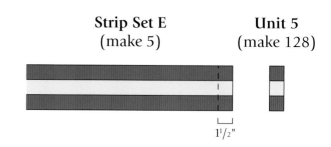

1½"

6. Sew 1 red **narrow strip** and 1 white **narrow strip** together to make **Strip Set F**. Make 5 **Strip Set F's**. Cut across Strip Set F's at 1¹/₂" intervals to make 128 **Unit 6's**.

Strip Set F
(make 5)

Unit 6
(make 128)

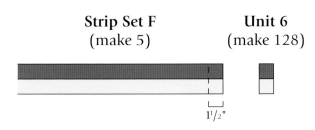

7. Sew 2 **Unit 1's** and 1 **Unit 3** together to make **Unit 7**. Make 16 **Unit 7's**.

Unit 7 (make 16)

8. Sew 1 **Unit 2** and 1 **Unit 3** together to make **Unit 8**. Make 64 **Unit 8's**.

Unit 8 (make 64)

9. Sew 2 **Unit 4's** and 1 **Unit 5** together to make **Unit 9**. Make 128 **Unit 9's**.

Unit 9 (make 128)

10. Sew 2 **Unit 6's** together to make **Unit 10**. Make 64 **Unit 10's**.

Unit 10 (make 64)

11. Sew 2 **Unit 10's**, 2 **small rectangles**, and 1 **Unit 8** together to make **Unit 11**. Make 32 **Unit 11's**.

Unit 11 (make 32)

12. Sew 2 **small rectangles**, 2 **Unit 9's**, and 1 **large rectangle** together to make **Unit 12**. Make 32 **Unit 12's**.

Unit 12 (make 32)

13. Sew 2 **Unit 8's**, 2 **large rectangles**, and 1 **Unit 7** together to make **Unit 13**. Make 16 **Unit 13's**.

Unit 13 (make 16)

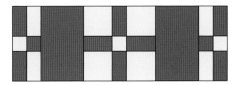

14. Sew 2 **Unit 11's**, 2 **Unit 12's**, and 1 **Unit 13** together to make **Unit 14**. Make 16 **Unit 14's**.

Unit 14 (make 16)

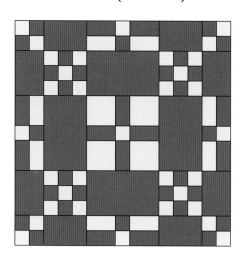

15. Sew 1 **border strip** and 2 **Unit 9's** together to make **Unit 15**. Make 32 **Unit 15's**.

Unit 15 (make 32)

16. Sew 1 **border strip** to opposite sides of **Unit 14** to make **Unit 16**. Make 16 **Unit 16's**.

Unit 16 (make 16)

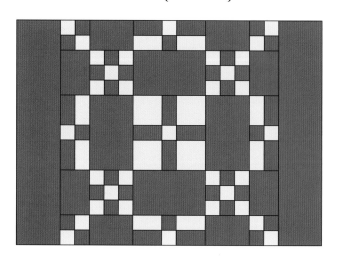

17. Sew 2 **Unit 15's** to remaining sides of **Unit 16** to make **Block**. Make 16 **Blocks**.

Block (make 16)

18. Sew 4 **Blocks** together to make **Row 1**. Repeat to make **Rows 2-4**.

Row 1

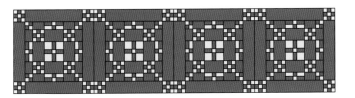

19. Match seamlines between blocks and sew **Row 1** to **Row 2**. Repeat to add **Rows 3** and 4 to complete **Quilt Top**.

completing the quilt

1. Follow **Quilting**, page 88, to mark, layer, and quilt, using **Quilting Diagram** as a suggestion. Use **Quilting Patterns**, page 81, if desired, reversing pattern as necessary. Our quilt is hand quilted.
2. Cut a 33" square of binding fabric. Follow **Making Continuous Bias Strip Binding**, page 93, to make $2^{1}/_{2}$"w bias binding.
3. Follow **Attaching Binding With Mitered Corners**, page 94, to attach binding to quilt.

Quilting Diagram

Quilt Top Diagram

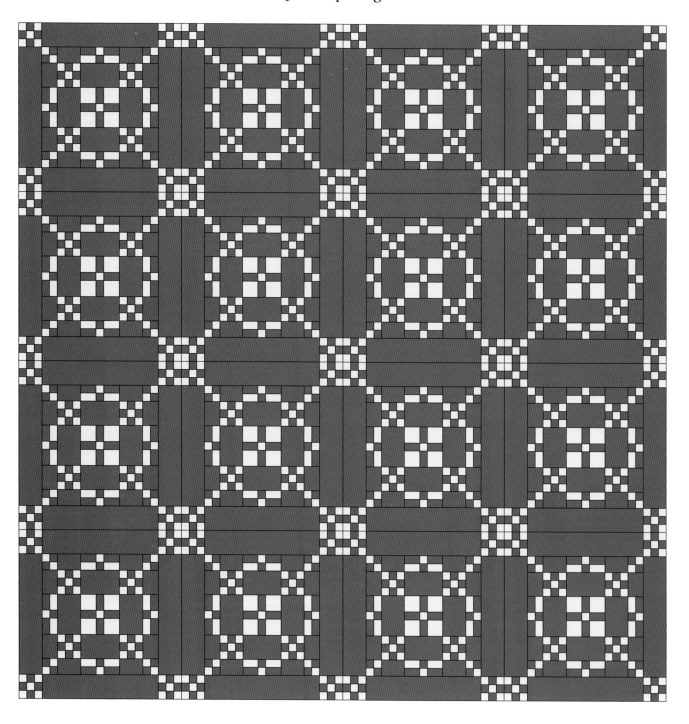

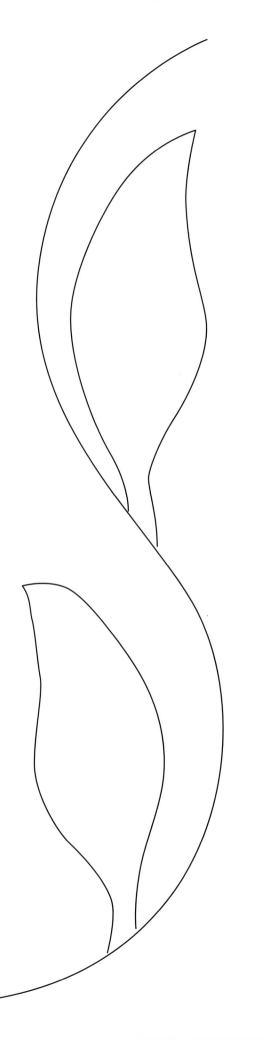

Burgoyne Surrounded
Quilting Patterns

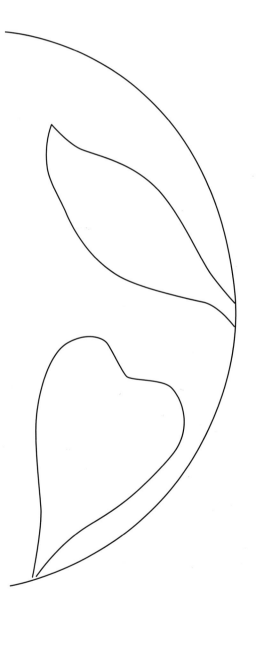

Crown of Thorns Quilt
Quilting Pattern

Crown of Thorns Quilt
Quilting Pattern

Crown of Thorns Quilt
Quilting Pattern

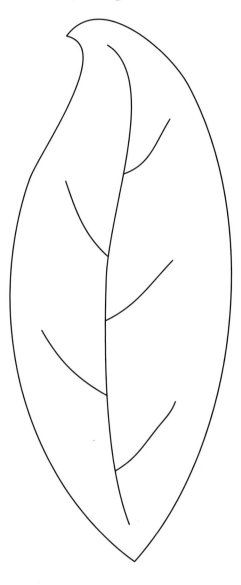

Chinese Coins Quilt
Feather Template
Pattern

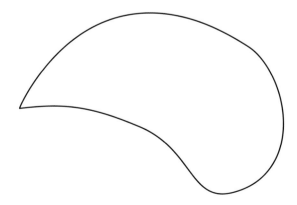

Chinese Coins Quilt
Cable Pattern

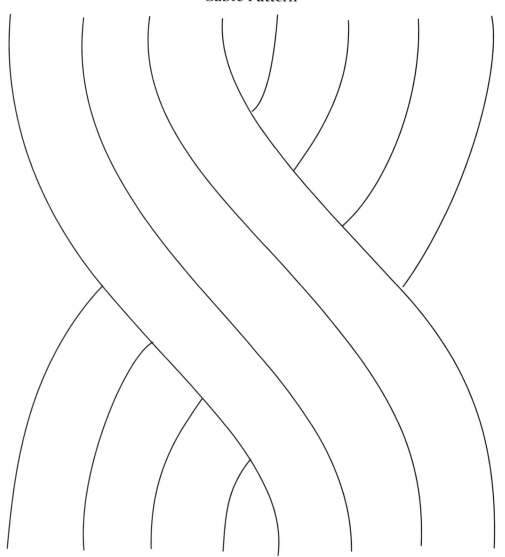

Metric Conversion Chart		
Inches x 2.54 = centimeters (cm)	Yards x .9144 = meters (m)	
Inches x 25.4 = millimeters (mm)	Yards x 91.44 = centimeters (cm)	
Inches x .0254 = meters (m)	Centimeters x .3937 = inches (")	
	Meters x 1.0936 = yards (yd)	

Standard Equivalents

⅛"	3.2 mm	0.32 cm	⅛ yard	11.43 cm	0.11 m
¼"	6.35 mm	0.635 cm	¼ yard	22.86 cm	0.23 m
⅜"	9.5 mm	0.95 cm	⅜ yard	34.29 cm	0.34 m
½"	12.7 mm	1.27 cm	½ yard	45.72 cm	0.46 m
⅝"	15.9 mm	1.59 cm	⅝ yard	57.15 cm	0.57 m
¾"	19.1 mm	1.91 cm	¾ yard	68.58 cm	0.69 m
⅞"	22.2 mm	2.22 cm	⅞ yard	80 cm	0.8 m
1 "	25.4 mm	2.54 cm	1 yard	91.44 cm	0.91 m

general instructions

To make your quilting easier and more enjoyable, we encourage you to carefully read all of the general instructions, study the color photographs, and familiarize yourself with the individual project instructions before beginning a project.

fabrics

selecting fabrics

Choose high-quality, medium-weight 100% cotton fabrics. All-cotton fabrics hold a crease better, fray less, and are easier to quilt than cotton/polyester blends.

Yardage requirements listed for each project are based on 43"/44" wide fabric with a "usable" width of 40" after shrinkage and trimming selvages. Actual usable width will probably vary slightly from fabric to fabric. Our recommended yardage lengths should be adequate for occasional re-squaring of fabric when many cuts are required.

preparing fabrics

We recommend that all fabrics be washed, dried, and pressed before cutting. If fabrics are not pre-washed, washing the finished quilt will cause shrinkage and give it a more "antiqued" look and feel. Bright and dark colors, which may run, should always be washed before cutting. After washing and drying fabric, fold lengthwise with wrong sides together and matching selvages.

rotary cutting

Rotary cutting has brought speed and accuracy to quiltmaking by allowing quilters to easily cut strips of fabric and then cut those strips into smaller pieces.

- Place fabric on work surface with fold closest to you.

- Cut all strips from the selvage-to-selvage width of the fabric unless otherwise indicated in project instructions.

- Square left edge of fabric using rotary cutter and rulers (**Figs. 1 - 2**).

Fig. 1   **Fig. 2**

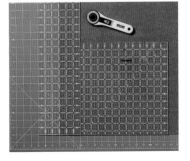 

- To cut each strip required for a project, place ruler over cut edge of fabric, aligning desired marking on ruler with cut edge; make cut (**Fig. 3**).

Fig. 3

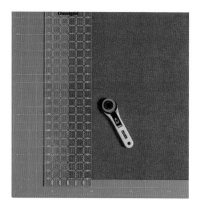

- When cutting several strips from a single piece of fabric, it is important to make sure that cuts remain at a perfect right angle to the fold; square fabric as needed.

piecing

Precise cutting, followed by accurate piecing, will ensure that all pieces of quilt top fit together well.

hand piecing

- Use ruler and sharp fabric marking pencil to draw all seam lines and transfer any alignment markings onto back of cut pieces.

- Matching right sides, pin two pieces together, using pins to mark corners.

- Use Running Stitch to sew pieces together along drawn line, backstitching at beginning and end of seam.

- Do not extend stitches into seam allowances.

- Run five or six stitches onto needle before pulling needle through fabric.

- To add stability, backstitch every $3/4$" to 1".

machine piecing

- Set sewing machine stitch length for approximately 11 stitches per inch.

- Use neutral-colored general-purpose sewing thread (not quilting thread) in needle and in bobbin.

- An accurate $1/4$" seam allowance is *essential*. Presser feet that are $1/4$" wide are available for most sewing machines.

- When piecing, always place pieces right sides together and match raw edges; pin if necessary.

- Chain piecing saves time and will usually result in more accurate piecing.

- Trim away points of seam allowances that extend beyond edges of sewn pieces.

sewing strip sets

When there are several strips to assemble into a strip set, first sew strips together into pairs, then sew pairs together to form strip set. To help avoid distortion, sew seams in opposite directions (**Fig. 4**).

Fig. 4

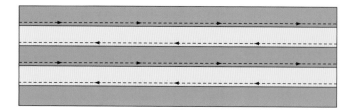

sewing across seam intersections

When sewing across intersection of two seams, place pieces right sides together and match seams exactly, making sure seam allowances are pressed in opposite directions (**Fig. 5**).

Fig. 5

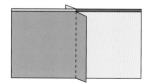

sewing sharp points

To ensure sharp points when joining triangular or diagonal pieces, stitch across the center of the "X" (shown in pink) formed on wrong side by previous seams (**Fig. 6**).

Fig. 6

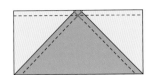

pressing

- Use steam iron set on "Cotton" for all pressing.

- Press after sewing each seam.

- Seam allowances are almost always pressed to one side, usually toward darker fabric. However, to reduce bulk it may occasionally be necessary to press seam allowances toward the lighter fabric or even to press them open.

- To prevent dark fabric seam allowance from showing through light fabric, trim darker seam allowance slightly narrower than lighter seam allowance.

- To press long seams, such as those in long strip sets, without curving or other distortion, lay strips across width of the ironing board.

borders

Borders cut along the lengthwise grain will lay flatter and smoother than borders cut along the crosswise grain. Lengthwise-grain borders are especially important for bed-size quilts, since the more stable lengthwise grain is less likely to stretch out of shape and cause wavy edges. Our instructions for cutting borders for bed-size quilts also include an extra 2" at each end for "insurance"; borders will be trimmed after measuring completed center section of quilt top. And, as always, you should match right sides and raw edges and use a 1/4" seam allowance when sewing.

adding squared borders

1. Mark the center of each edge of quilt top.
2. Squared borders are usually added to top and bottom, then side edges, of the center section of a quilt top. To add top border, measure across center of quilt top to determine length of border (**Fig. 7**). Trim border to the determined length.

Fig. 7

3. Mark center of 1 long edge of border. Matching center marks and raw edges, pin border to quilt top, easing in any fullness; stitch.
4. Repeat Steps 2 and 3 to add bottom border to quilt top.
5. Measure center of quilt top (including attached borders) to determine length of side borders. Repeat Steps 2 and 3 to add side borders to quilt top (**Fig. 8**).

Fig. 8

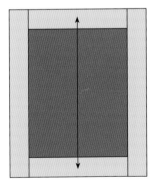

adding mitered borders

1. Mark the center of each edge of quilt top (see **Fig. 7**).
2. Mark center of 1 long edge of top border. Measure across center of quilt top (see **Fig. 7**). Matching center marks and raw edges, pin border to center of quilt top edge. From center of border, measure out ¹/₂ the width of the quilt top in both directions and mark. Match marks on border with corners of quilt top and pin. Easing in any fullness, pin border to quilt top between center and corners. Sew border to quilt top, beginning and ending seams exactly ¹/₄" from each corner of quilt top and backstitching at beginning and end of stitching (**Fig. 9**).

Fig. 9

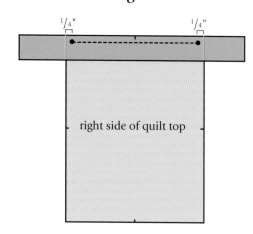

3. Repeat Step 2 to sew bottom, then side borders, to center section of quilt top. To temporarily move first 2 borders out of the way, fold and pin ends as shown in **Fig. 10**.

Fig. 10

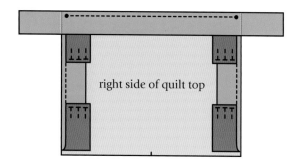

4. Fold 1 corner of quilt top diagonally with right sides together; use rotary cutting ruler to mark stitching line as shown in **Fig. 11**. Pin strips together along drawn line. Sew on drawn line, backstitching at beginning and end of stitching (**Fig. 12**).

Fig. 11	**Fig. 12**

5. Turn mitered corner right side up. Check to see that there is not a gap at the inner end of the seam and that corner does not pucker.
6. Trim seam allowances to ¹/₄"; press to 1 side.
7. Repeat Steps 4-6 to miter each remaining corner.

quilting

*Quilting holds the three layers (top, batting, and backing) of the quilt together and can be done by hand or machine. Because marking, layering, and quilting are interrelated and may be done in different orders depending on circumstances, please read entire **Quilting** section, pages 88 – 92, before beginning project.*

types of quilting designs

in the ditch quilting

Quilting along seamlines or along edges of appliquéd pieces is called "in the ditch" quilting. This type of quilting should be done on side **opposite** seam allowance and does not have to be marked.

outline quilting

Quilting a consistent distance, usually ¹/₄", from seam or appliqué is called "outline" quilting. Outline quilting may be marked, or ¹/₄" masking tape may be placed along seamlines for quilting guide. (Do not leave tape on quilt longer than necessary, since it may leave an adhesive residue.)

motif quilting

Quilting a design, such as a feathered wreath, is called "motif" quilting. This type of quilting should be marked before basting quilt layers together.

echo quilting

Quilting that follows the outline of an appliquéd or pieced design with two or more parallel lines is called "echo" quilting. This type of quilting does not need to be marked.

channel quilting

Quilting with straight, parallel lines is called "channel" quilting. This type of quilting may be marked or stitched using a guide.

crosshatch quilting

Quilting straight lines in a grid pattern is called "crosshatch" quilting. Lines may be stitched parallel to edges of quilt or stitched diagonally. This type of quilting may be marked or stitched using a guide.

meandering quilting

Quilting in random curved lines and swirls is called "meandering" quilting. Quilting lines should not cross or touch each other. This type of quilting does not need to be marked.

stipple quilting

Meandering quilting that is very closely spaced is called "stipple" quilting. Stippling will flatten the area quilted and is often stitched in background areas to raise appliquéd or pieced designs. This type of quilting does not need to be marked.

marking quilting lines

Quilting lines may be marked using fabric marking pencils, chalk markers, water- or air-soluble pens, or lead pencils.

Simple quilting designs may be marked with chalk or chalk pencil after basting. A small area may be marked, then quilted, before moving to next area to be marked. Intricate designs should be marked before basting using a more durable marker.

Caution: Pressing may permanently set some marks. **Test** different markers **on scrap fabric** to find one that marks clearly and can be thoroughly removed.

A wide variety of pre-cut quilting stencils, as well as entire books of quilting patterns, are available. Using a stencil makes it easier to mark intricate or repetitive designs.

To make a stencil from a pattern, center template plastic over pattern and use a permanent marker to trace pattern onto plastic. Use a craft knife with single or double blade to cut channels along traced lines (**Fig. 13**).

Fig. 13

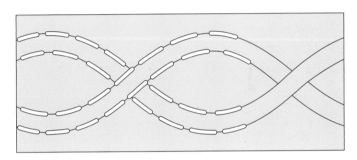

preparing the backing

To allow for slight shifting of quilt top during quilting, backing should be approximately 4" larger on all sides. Yardage requirements listed for quilt backings are calculated for 43"/44"w fabric. Using 90"w or 108"w fabric for the backing of a bed-sized quilt may eliminate piecing. To piece a backing using 43"/44"w fabric, use the following instructions.

1. Measure length and width of quilt top; add 8" to each measurement.

2. If determined width is 79" or less, cut backing fabric into two lengths slightly longer than determined *length* measurement. Trim selvages. Place lengths with right sides facing and sew long edges together, forming tube (**Fig. 14**). Match seams and press along one fold (**Fig. 15**). Cut along pressed fold to form single piece (**Fig. 16**).

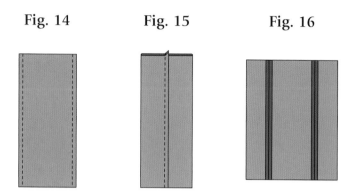

| **Fig. 14** | **Fig. 15** | **Fig. 16** |

3. If determined width is more than 79", it may require less fabric yardage if the backing is pieced horizontally. Divide determined *length* measurement by 40" to determine how many widths will be needed. Cut required number of widths the determined *width* measurement. Trim selvages. Sew long edges together to form single piece.

4. Trim backing to size determined in Step 1; press seam allowances open.

choosing the batting

The appropriate batting will make quilting easier. For fine hand quilting, choose low-loft batting. All cotton or cotton/polyester blend battings work well for machine quilting because the cotton helps "grip" quilt layers. If quilt is to be tied, a high-loft batting, sometimes called extra-loft or fat batting, may be used to make quilt "fluffy."

Types of batting include cotton, polyester, wool, cotton/polyester blend, cotton/wool blend, and silk.

When selecting batting, refer to package labels for characteristics and care instructions. Cut batting same size as prepared backing.

assembling the quilt

1. Examine wrong side of quilt top closely; trim any seam allowances and clip any threads that may show through front of the quilt. Press quilt top, being careful not to "set" any marked quilting lines.

2. Place backing *wrong* side up on flat surface. Use masking tape to tape edges of backing to surface. Place batting on top of backing fabric. Smooth batting gently, being careful not to stretch or tear. Center quilt top *right* side up on batting.

3. If hand quilting, begin in center and work toward outer edges to hand baste all layers together. Use long stitches and place basting lines approximately 4" apart (**Fig. 17**). Smooth fullness or wrinkles toward outer edges.

Fig. 17

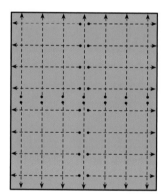

4. If machine quilting, use 1" rustproof safety pins to "pin-baste" all layers together, spacing pins approximately 4" apart. Begin at center and work toward outer edges to secure all layers. If possible, place pins away from areas that will be quilted, although pins may be removed as needed when quilting.

hand quilting

The quilting stitch is a basic running stitch that forms a broken line on quilt top and backing. Stitches on quilt top and backing should be straight and equal in length.

1. Secure center of quilt in hoop or frame. Check quilt top and backing to make sure they are smooth. To help prevent puckers, always begin quilting in the center of quilt and work toward outside edges.

2. Thread needle with 18" - 20" length of quilting thread; knot one end. Using thimble, insert needle into quilt top and batting approximately ¹/₂" from quilting line. Bring needle up on quilting line (**Fig. 18**); when knot catches on quilt top, give thread a quick, short pull to "pop" knot through fabric into batting (**Fig. 19**).

Fig. 18   **Fig. 19**

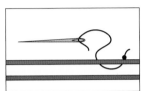   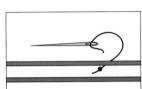

3. Holding needle with sewing hand and placing other hand underneath quilt, use thimble to push tip of needle down through all layers. As soon as needle touches finger underneath, use that finger to push tip of needle only back up through layers to top of quilt. (The amount of needle showing above fabric determines length of quilting stitch.) Referring to **Fig. 20**, rock needle up and down, taking three to six stitches before bringing needle and thread completely through layers. Check back of quilt to make sure stitches are going through all layers. If necessary, make one stitch at a time when quilting through seam allowances or along curves and corners.

Fig. 20

4. At end of thread, knot thread close to fabric and "pop" knot into batting; clip thread close to fabric.
5. Move hoop as often as necessary. Thread may be left dangling and picked up again after returning to that part of quilt.

machine quilting methods

Use general-purpose thread in bobbin. Do not use quilting thread. Thread the needle of machine with general-purpose thread or transparent monofilament thread to make quilting blend with quilt top fabrics. Use decorative thread, such as a metallic or contrasting-color general-purpose thread, to make quilting lines stand out more.

straight-line quilting
The term "straight-line" is somewhat deceptive, since curves (especially gentle ones) as well as straight lines can be stitched with this technique.

1. Set stitch length for six to ten stitches per inch and attach walking foot to sewing machine.
2. Determine which section of quilt will have longest continuous quilting line, oftentimes area from center top to center bottom. Roll up and secure each edge of quilt to help reduce the bulk, keeping fabrics smooth. Smaller projects may not need to be rolled.
3. Begin stitching on longest quilting line, using very short stitches for the first ¹/₄" to "lock" quilting. Stitch across project, using one hand on each side of walking foot to slightly spread fabric and to guide fabric through machine. Lock stitches at end of quilting line.
4. Continue machine quilting, stitching longer quilting lines first to stabilize quilt before moving on to other areas.

free-motion quilting
Free-motion quilting may be free form or may follow a marked pattern.

1. Attach darning foot to sewing machine and lower or cover feed dogs.
2. Position quilt under darning foot; lower foot. Holding top thread, take a stitch and pull bobbin thread to top of quilt. To "lock" beginning of quilting line, hold top and bobbin threads while making three to five stitches in place.

3. Use one hand on each side of darning foot to slightly spread fabric and to move fabric through the machine. Even stitch length is achieved by using smooth, flowing hand motion and steady machine speed. Slow machine speed and fast hand movement will create long stitches. Fast machine speed and slow hand movement will create short stitches. Move quilt sideways, back and forth, in a circular motion, or in a random motion to create desired designs; do not rotate quilt. Lock stitches at end of each quilting line.

tying a quilt

Tied quilts use yarn or floss ties instead of quilting stitches to secure the layers. For a tied quilt, be sure to use bonded batting to prevent separation or bunching when the quilt is laundered. You may also use a higher loft batting than when quilting.

1. Determine where ties will be placed and mark if necessary. Space ties evenly. On a pieced top, tie at corners of blocks or pieces within blocks.
2. Follow **Preparing The Backing**, page 89, and **Assembling the Quilt**, page 90, to prepare quilt for tying.
3. Thread a large darning needle with a long length of embroidery floss, yarn, or pearl cotton; do not knot.
4. At each mark or tie location, take a small stitch through all layers of quilt. Pull up floss, but do not cut between stitches (**Fig. 21**). Begin at center of quilt and work toward outside edges, rethreading needle as necessary.

Fig. 21

5. Cut floss between stitches. At each stitch, use a square knot to tie floss securely (**Fig. 22**); trim ties to desired length.

Fig. 22

making a hanging sleeve

Attaching a hanging sleeve to back of wall hanging or quilt before the binding is added allows project to be displayed on wall.

1. Measure width of quilt top edge and subtract 1". Cut piece of fabric 7"w by determined measurement.
2. Press short edges of fabric piece $^1/_4$" to wrong side; press edges $^1/_4$" to wrong side again and machine stitch in place.
3. Matching wrong sides, fold piece in half lengthwise to form tube.
4. Follow project instructions to sew binding to quilt top and to trim backing and batting. Before Blindstitching binding to backing, match raw edges and stitch hanging sleeve to center top edge on back of quilt.
5. Finish binding quilt, treating hanging sleeve as part of backing.
6. Blindstitch bottom of hanging sleeve to backing, taking care not to stitch through to front of quilt.

binding

Binding encloses the raw edges of quilt. Because of its stretchiness, bias binding works well for binding projects with curves or rounded corners and tends to lie smooth and flat in any given circumstance. Binding may also be cut from straight lengthwise or crosswise grain of fabric.

making continuous bias strip binding

Bias strips for binding can simply be cut and pieced to desired length. However, when a long length of binding is needed, the "continuous" method is quick and accurate.

1. Cut square from binding fabric the size indicated in project instructions. Cut square in half diagonally to make two triangles.
2. With right sides together and using $1/4$" seam allowance, sew triangles together (**Fig. 23**); press seam allowances open.

Fig. 23

3. On wrong side of fabric, draw lines the width of binding as specified in project instructions, usually $2^{1}/_{2}$" (**Fig. 24**). Cut off any remaining fabric less than this width.

Fig. 24

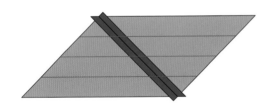

4. With right sides inside, bring short edges together to form tube; match raw edges so that first drawn line of top section meets second drawn line of bottom section (**Fig. 25**).

Fig. 25

5. Carefully pin edges together by inserting pins through drawn lines at point where drawn lines intersect, making sure pins go through intersections on both sides. Using $1/4$" seam allowance, sew edges together; press seam allowances open.
6. To cut continuous strip, begin cutting along first drawn line (**Fig. 26**). Continue cutting along drawn line around tube.

Fig. 26

7. Trim ends of bias strip square.
8. Matching wrong sides and raw edges, carefully press bias strip in half lengthwise to complete binding.

making straight-grain binding

1. To determine length of strip needed if attaching binding with mitered corners, measure edges of quilt and add 12".
2. To determine lengths of strips needed if attaching binding with overlapped corners, measure each edge of quilt; add 3" to each measurement.
3. Cut lengthwise or crosswise strips of binding fabric the determined length and the width called for in project instructions. Strips may be pieced using diagonal seams to achieve necessary length.
4. Matching wrong sides and raw edges, press strip(s) in half lengthwise to complete binding.

attaching binding with mitered corners

1. Beginning with one end near center on bottom edge of quilt, lay binding around quilt to make sure that seams in binding will not end up at a corner. Adjust placement if necessary. Matching raw edges of binding to raw edge of quilt top, pin binding to right side of quilt along one edge.

2. When you reach first corner, mark ¹/₄" from corner of quilt top (**Fig. 27**).

Fig. 27

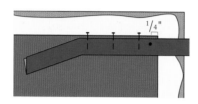

3. Beginning approximately 10" from end of binding and using ¹/₄" seam allowance, sew binding to quilt, backstitching at beginning of stitching and at mark (**Fig. 28**). Lift needle out of fabric and clip thread.

Fig. 28

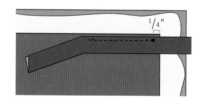

4. Fold binding as shown in **Figs. 29 – 30** and pin binding to adjacent side, matching raw edges. When you've reached the next corner, mark ¹/₄" from edge of quilt top.

Fig. 29   **Fig. 30**

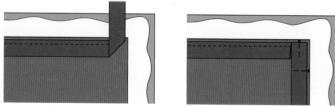

5. Backstitching at edge of quilt top, sew pinned binding to quilt (**Fig. 31**); backstitch at the next mark. Lift needle out of fabric and clip thread.

Fig. 31

6. Continue sewing binding to quilt, stopping approximately 10" from starting point (**Fig. 32**).

Fig. 32

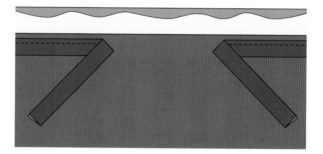

7. Bring beginning and end of binding to center of opening and fold each end back, leaving a ¹/₄" space between folds (**Fig. 33**). Finger press folds.

Fig. 33

8. Unfold ends of binding and draw a line across wrong side in finger-pressed crease. Draw a line through the lengthwise pressed fold of binding at the same spot to create a cross mark. With edge of ruler at cross mark, line up 45° angle marking on ruler with one long side of binding. Draw a diagonal line from edge to edge. Repeat on remaining end, making sure that the two diagonal lines are angled the same way (**Fig. 34**).

Fig. 34

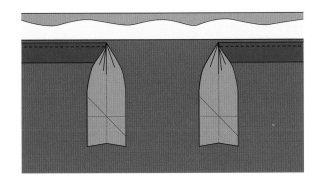

9. Matching right sides and diagonal lines, pin binding ends together at right angles (**Fig. 35**).

Fig. 35

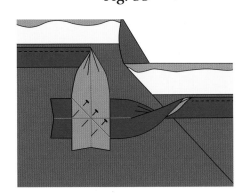

10. Machine stitch along diagonal line (**Fig. 36**), removing pins as you stitch.

Fig. 36

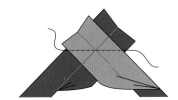

11. Lay binding against quilt to double check that it is correct length.
12. Trim binding ends, leaving $^1/_4$" seam allowance; press seam open. Stitch binding to quilt.
13. Trim backing and batting a scant $^1/_4$" larger than quilt top so that batting and backing will fill the binding when it is folded over to quilt backing.
14. On one edge of quilt, fold binding over to quilt backing and pin pressed edge in place, covering stitching line (**Fig. 37**). On adjacent side, fold binding over, forming a mitered corner (**Fig. 38**). Repeat to pin remainder of binding in place.

Fig. 37

Fig. 38

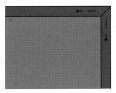

15. Blindstitch binding to backing, taking care not to stitch through to front of quilt.

attaching binding with overlapped corners

1. Matching raw edges and using 1/4" seam allowance, sew a length of binding to top and bottom edges on right side of quilt.

2. Trim backing and batting a scant 1/4" larger than quilt top so that batting and backing will fill the binding when it is folded over to quilt backing.

3. Trim ends of top and bottom binding even with edges of quilt top. Fold binding over to quilt backing and pin pressed edges in place, covering stitching line (**Fig. 39**); blindstitch binding to backing.

Fig. 39

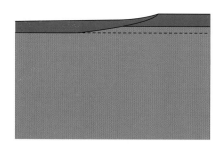

4. Leaving approximately 1 1/2" of binding at each end, stitch a length of binding to each side edge of quilt. Trim backing and batting as in Step 2.

5. Trim each end of binding 1/2" longer than bound edge. Fold each end of binding over to quilt backing (**Fig. 40**); pin in place. Fold binding over to quilt backing and blindstitch in place, taking care not to stitch through to front of quilt.

Fig. 40

blind stitch

Come up at 1, go down at 2, and come up at 3 (**Fig. 41**). Length of stitches may be varied as desired.

Fig. 41

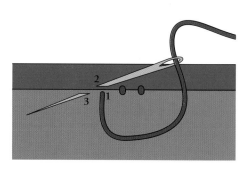

signing and dating your quilt

A completed quilt is a work of art and should be signed and dated. There are many different ways to do this and numerous books on the subject. The label should reflect the style of the quilt, the occasion or person for which it was made, and the quilter's own particular talents. Following are suggestions for recording the history of quilt or adding a sentiment for future generations.

- Embroider quilter's name, date, and any additional information on quilt top or backing. Matching floss, such as cream floss on white border, will leave a subtle record. Bright or contrasting floss will make the information stand out.

- Make label from muslin and use permanent marker to write information. Use different colored permanent markers to make label more decorative. Stitch label to back of quilt.

- Use photo-transfer paper to add image to white or cream fabric label. Stitch label to back of quilt.

- Piece an extra block from quilt top pattern to use as label. Add information with permanent fabric pen. Appliqué block to back of quilt.

- Write message on appliquéd design from quilt top. Attach appliqué to back of the quilt.